Active Directory® Forestry

Investigating and Managing Objects and Attributes for Microsoft® Windows® 2000 and Microsoft® Windows® Server 2003

– A Geek's Guide

John Craddock and Sally Storey

Investigating and Managing Objects and Attributes
for Microsoft® Windows® 2000 and Windows® Server 2003

A Geek's Guide

© 2003 John Craddock and Sally Storey

Illustrator: Sally L Hall

A CIP catalogue record for this book is available from the British Library.

ISBN 0-9544218-0-9

Printing history: January 2003, first edition

Published by: Kimberry Associates, PO Box 38638, London, W13 8WQ

Table of Contents

Chapter 1 – What and Why

What is this book about?

This book peels back the covers on Active Directory® and provides you with the technical in-depth details of objects and attributes and how they interact. The book centres around our Geek's Reference (Chapter 3) which provides an in-depth explanation of the key objects and attributes in a clear and precise manner. Explanations are backed up with solid working examples showing you how to interrogate the directory using the Microsoft support tool LDP. The majority of techniques that we show you apply equally well to the Microsoft® Windows® 2000 Server and Microsoft® Windows® Server 2003 families.

Our testing has been performed using the RC1 build of Microsoft® Windows® .NET Server 2003 and we don't anticipate any significant functional changes in the final release.

Now, we all like a challenge… As the presses were about to roll with the first print run, Microsoft announced the product name change from Microsoft® Windows® .NET Server 2003 to Microsoft® Windows® Server 2003. Whilst we have changed all product references, we cannot be certain if any programmatic variable references will be impacted by the name change. For example .NET forest functionality may well be renamed to 2003 forest functionality. We have a bet running on this! For the moment, we have kept the current names and our wagers are in the corner!

LDP allows you to create native Lightweight Directory Access Protocol (LDAP) commands to query and modify the Active Directory®. Through the use of this powerful support tool, if you have the right credentials, you will be able to gain access and effect change to all objects and attributes within the Active Directory®.

This book provides you with the skills you need to perform in-depth investigations into the directory. An essential companion if you are troubleshooting or responding to change requests.

Discover how to...
- Display deleted directory objects
- Create or modify any type of object
- Check if an attribute is indexed
- Locate the security principal for an unknown account
- Examine which attributes are published in the global catalog
- Investigate which attributes are members of the ANR set
- Test individual bits within an attribute
- Gain ultimate access to the Active Directory®

Why have we written this book?

The Active Directory® publishes information about data and services available throughout your enterprise. Your business systems will be dependant on you establishing and maintaining a rock solid infrastructure. There are many texts on designing and deploying the Active Directory®. These texts describe how to create and maintain objects and their associated attributes through the standard user interface tools, but what if you need to go beyond that?

Your systems are dependant on the correct representation of resources within the directory.
- If an application is regularly searching for an attribute value, that value should be indexed. How do you know which attributes are indexed?
- Property sets allow you to configure security on a number of attributes through a single Access Control Entry (ACE). How do you know which attributes are members of a property set?
- If you want to perform enterprise-wide searches for a particular attribute value, that value needs to be in the global catalog (GC). How do you know which attributes are published to the global catalog?

We've often heard the complaint from system administrators, architects and programmers that they cannot find this information documented.

You could argue that it would be irresponsible for Microsoft® to document much of this because it could be conceived as complete. The directory is totally extensible and dynamic so any documentation apart from your own will invariably be out of date. Directory-enabled applications will change the number of indexed attributes, members of a property set and so on.

You have to be able to document your own Active Directory® and that's why we wrote this book.

We believe that LDP was written for geeks, nerds and the initiated and to maximise its use, you need solid LDAP skills. This book comes to the rescue. It provides a comprehensive guide to using LDP without having to be a master guru in LDAP.

Who is this book for?

It is for anyone who wants to dig deep into the Active Directory®, including:
- System administrators
- System architects
- Support engineers
- Programmers writing directory enabled applications

The book will aid you in solving complex administration tasks and Active Directory® troubleshooting. The book assumes that you are familiar with Active Directory® concepts to a fairly advanced level. On our geekometer scale this book is extreme!

A really important warning

If you use the ADSI Edit snap-in, the LDP utility or any other LDAP client and incorrectly modify the Active Directory® you could cause serious problems. This may cause you loss of data and require you to reinstall the operating system and applications. It cannot be guaranteed that problems resulting from the incorrect modification of the Active Directory® can be solved. Make modifications at your own risk in a test environment before applying them to any production system.

How to use this book

To gain full benefit from the book start at the beginning and work your way through to the end. We strongly advise you to try out all the examples in a test forest – our test environment is documented in Appendix A. If you choose not to use our test forest naming conventions, you will need to modify the examples as appropriate. It is important that LDP is configured correctly and if you are unsuccessful at any point refer to the section on setting the initial search conditions in Chapter 5.

If you are:

- In a hurry and need an introduction, start with Chapter 2 which introduces Active Directory® objects and attributes. After that, dip in and out as necessary, referring to the table of contents and the index.
- In need of further explanation, refer to the Active Directory® Geek's Reference in Chapter 3. You will find our ultimate reference to the key objects, attributes and concepts.
- If you are new to LDP, work through the LDP Primer in Chapter 4.
- If you are trying to solve a particular problem, refer to the comprehensive indexing.

Syntax and naming conventions

Where object and attribute names have been individually mentioned in the text, they are italicised. The majority of names used are the LDAP display names as these are the names you need when programmatically accessing the directory.

Feedback and comments

If you would like to contribute your feedback, comments or questions, please contact us at O&Acomments@kimberry.co.uk.

Thank you for taking the time to buy this book and letting us know what you think. If you have suggestions for future books, we would like to hear.

Chapter 2 – Active Directory® Objects and Attributes

Before we start, let's set the scene

The Active Directory® is just a container that holds a bunch of objects. These objects are used to logically represent resources within your enterprise (users, computers, printers, sites and much more...). Each object consists of a set of attributes. These attributes contain data values that define the characteristics and behaviour of a particular resource. You can think of an object as being represented by a row within a database with attribute values held in columns. When you modify an object in the directory you are actually modifying the object's attributes. When you search the directory, you will be searching for attributes that are set to a particular value.

When an object is created in the Active Directory® it is "publishing" information about the resource. Users and administrators can locate resources simply by searching the Active Directory®. Designed correctly, the Active Directory® can be used to logically represent an enterprise environment in a manner that is ideal for both users and administrators.

The design should appropriately group objects that require controlling in a common way. The objects are grouped within Organisational Units (OUs) and controlled via the application of group policy and object security. Object security controls visibility and administrative access to the objects, but here we digress, this is a subject for another book...

You will require the appropriate documentation about objects, attributes and their associated values to perform advance administration, troubleshooting and resolution of Active Directory® problems. Trawling the web and other resources to find this information can be tedious, time consuming and terrifically frustrating. Most likely, the information you need to solve your problem is held in your directory, all you need to know is how to read it!

The on-the-wire protocol that is used to access the directory is LDAP. LDAP commands can be used to create, delete, locate and modify Active Directory® objects, attributes and values. Through the use of the LDP support tool we will show you how to gain access to the directory using LDAP.

But before we start you need to know how objects and attributes are defined and named.

The Schema

The schema provides the formal definition of all objects and attributes in the directory. You can consider the schema as the ultimate documentation for directory objects and attributes. In this section we will introduce the main schema concepts. This book does not cover full details of the schema.

A directory object is used to represent some entity (thing). For example a user account object represents users; and a computer account object represents computers. Each type of directory object is defined in the schema. The formal definition of an object is called an object class definition. There are object classes defined for all the different types of objects that can be created in the directory. A newly installed Active Directory® has a number of predefined object classes, 142 on Microsoft® Windows® 2000 and 189 on Microsoft® Windows® Server. The schema is extensible and new class definitions can be created as necessary to represent additional entities. Active Directory® applications such as Microsoft® Exchange 2000 extend the schema by adding new object classes that are required to represent their entities.

An object class defines a set of attributes that are required to represent the entity; the attributes define the characteristics of the entity. For example a user object class will consist of a number of attributes that define a user object such as:

- given name
- surname
- description
- logon account name
- SID
- home directory

When an object is created in the directory certain attributes (mandatory attributes) must be populated with values. Populating other attributes is optional. Which attributes are mandatory and which are optional are defined as part of the object class definition in the schema.

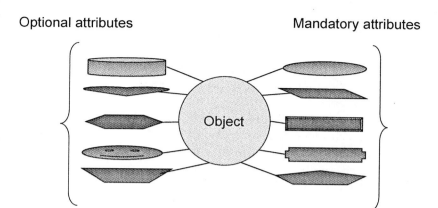

Optional attributes   **Mandatory attributes**

Figure 2.1 – Mandatory and optional attributes

Object classes can have a number of attributes in common. Rather than adding these attributes to each object class definition, definitions can be derived from other classes. An object class will have all the attributes of its parent class in addition to the attributes that are defined for the object itself. With the exception of the Top object class all objects are derived from other classes.

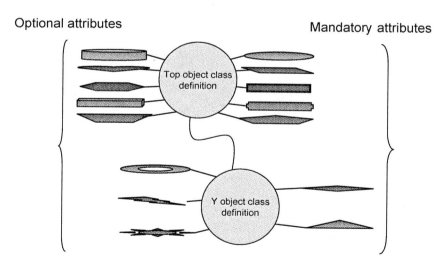

Optional attributes   **Mandatory attributes**

Figure 2.2 – Class derivation

When creating an instance of object Y in the directory, in addition to the mandatory attributes defined for the Y object class, all of the mandatory attributes defined for the Top object class must be populated. Similarly the optional attributes available to an instance of object Y are a concatenation of the optional attributes for both object classes.

The simplest analogy we can think of for the schema is a cake recipe book. The recipe book provides recipes for many different types of cakes (object classes) and each cake recipe is comprised of a set of ingredients (attributes).

In order to create our chosen cake, some of the ingredients such as flour, eggs and milk will be mandatory. Other ingredients however, such as candies and a Happy Birthday banner are optional. If the recipe book defines a base cake (top object class) other types of cakes (object classes) can be defined which use the base cake recipe and add additional ingredients to make them unique.

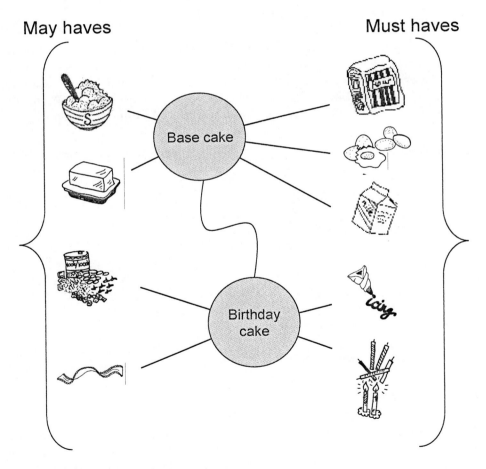

Figure 2.3 – Simple schema analogy

For consistency, when defining a new recipe it must conform to a standard format:

Name of cake class	Birthday
Derived from	Base cake
Must have ingredients	Icing, candles
May have ingredients	Candies, ribbon

If you look at this definition it is just a set of attributes: name of cake class, derived from, must have ingredients and may have ingredients. These specify the characteristics of the cake class object. A format for writing recipes could also be defined in the recipe book (schema) so that readers could create their own recipes in a standard way.

In the Active Directory® schema, all object classes are derived from a standard template which is defined as an object called *classSchema*.

Objects have attributes that define the characteristics of the object to which they belong. Attributes have their own attributes (we will call them properties) which define the characteristics of the attribute.

Examples of attribute properties are:
- common name
- syntax (format of the data that can be stored)
- allowed data range

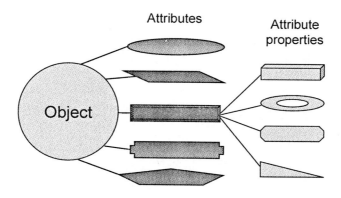

Figure 2.4 – Object attributes and attribute properties

Attributes are defined in the schema as *attributeSchema* objects.

Naming Objects

Directory objects are located using a unique Distinguished Name (DN). A Relative Distinguished Name (RDN) is defined as part of an objects creation. The DN of the object is a concatenation of the object's RDN and the RDN for each of the nodes in the object's path.

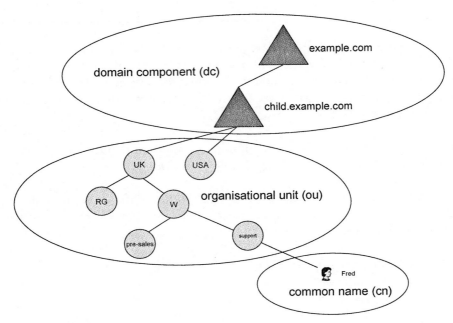

Figure 2.5 – Distinguished names

In this diagram the DN for the user account object Fred is:

cn=fred,ou=support,ou=w,ou=uk,dc=child,dc=example,dc=com

Each component (separated by a comma) in the above string specifies an RDN. The attribute used to store the RDN is defined in the schema and varies for different classes of objects.

- The RDN for a user object is stored in the Common-Name (*cn*) attribute.
- The RDN for an organization unit object is stored in the Organizational-Unit-Name (*ou*) attribute.
- The RDN for a domain object is stored in the Domain-Component (*dc*) attribute.

So how do you find out which attribute stores an object's RDN? See Chapter 3, Object Names.

In addition to a DN, every directory object is uniquely identified by a Globally Unique Identifier (GUID). Security principals such as users, groups and computers also have a Security Identifier (SID). The DN of an object will change if the object is renamed or moved, whereas the GUID will remain unchanged throughout the forest and the SID will remain unchanged within a domain.

When accessing an object you will need to uniquely identify it within the directory; it can be identified by its DN, GUID or in the case of a security principal, by its SID.

You will need to define a base from which to start searching the directory. This can be identified by DN, GUID or SID.

Naming Contexts

The Active Directory® is split into a number of Naming Contexts (NCs). Naming context is a X.500 term which identifies a partial subtree (partition) of the Directory Information Tree (DIT). NCs are individually replicated.

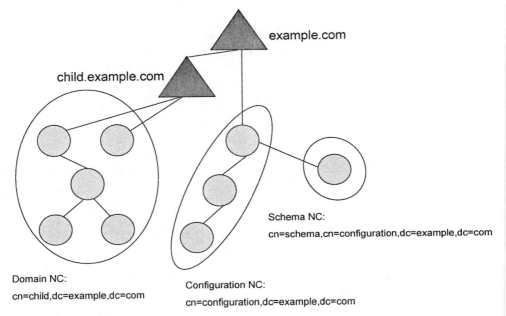

Figure 2.6 – Naming contexts

Both the schema and configuration naming contexts are replicated throughout the forest.

Schema Naming Context

The schema naming context contains all of the class definitions for both objects and attributes.

Configuration Naming Context

The configuration naming context contains information about the overall configuration of the forest. This includes details of the domains, domain controllers, sites and replication topology.

Domain Naming Context

The domain naming context contains objects that have been defined within the domain. These objects are only replicated to domain controllers that are part of the domain.

Global Catalog

The global catalog is not an NC (it is not replicated as a single entity). The GC holds information about all the objects and to do this it must "pull" domain NC information from all domains in the forest. The size of the GC database is constrained by restricting the number of attributes that it stores for each object. The attributes that are replicated to the GC are defined as part of the schema definition for the attribute.

Application Directory Partitions

Microsoft® Windows® Server Active Directory® allows the creation of additional naming contexts. These are referred to as Application Directory Partitions.

When a directory enabled application is installed on Microsoft® Windows® 2000 Server it will probably create objects within the configuration container. The objects are then replicated to all domain controllers within the forest. The advantage of using application directory partitions is that a new NC can be created so that the objects are only replicated to designated domain controllers.

Microsoft® Windows® Server 2003 DNS can make use of application directory partitions. DNS records can be created in a new DomainDnsZone NC which just replicates to DNS servers in the domain or a ForestDnsZone NC that replicates to all DNS servers in the forest. Microsoft® Windows® 2000 Active Directory® integrated DNS is also supported.

Let's start drilling down into the directory...

If you want more details on aspects of the directory refer to Chapter 3, Active Directory® Geek's Reference. If you can't wait to start digging into the directory jump straight to Chapter 4, LDP Primer and refer back to Chapter 3 as necessary.

Chapter 3 – Active Directory® Geek's Reference

In this chapter we provide a reference to many of the core features of the Active Directory®. Following the philosophy of our book the information is presented in a concise and succinct manner that provides you with the hard facts. Understanding the Active Directory® presents one of those chicken-and-eggs conundrums, understanding one piece involves knowledge of another and so on. Rather than repeating information we have indexed the topics alphabetically in this chapter allowing you to dip in and out as necessary. Most of the topics are supported with solid examples later in the book and we advise you to try these out.

If you need help locating a topic, use the content guide at the beginning of the book. If you require a deeper understanding of any of the topics, look for appropriate examples using LDP. You will find references to these in the text and in the index at the end of the book.

Ambiguous Name Resolution

Ambiguous Name Resolution (ANR) provides a method of specifying a single search string which is automatically tested against multiple attributes. The name of the associated object is returned if any of the attribute values match the specified search string. To increase the extent of the search, the search string has a wildcard automatically appended (jo★).

The advantage of ANR is that searches can be executed through a single interface without having to specify the actual attributes to be tested.

For example, a user can search the Active Directory® via the user shell Find People dialog. Any search string that is entered in the Name field is tested against members of the ANR set. The ANR set includes the *sn* (surname), *givenName* and *physicalDeliveryOfficeName* attributes amongst others. If any of the attribute values match the search string, the name of the associated user is returned.

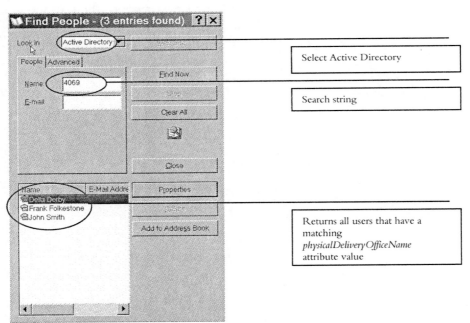

Figure 3.1 – Find People dialog showing ANR search

An ANR search can be performed through LDP by setting the search filter to (ANR=<search string>). The LDAP server converts the ANR search request into a complex LDAP query. You can see the filter expansion by enabling the Search Stats LDAP control. See Chapter 7, Controlling Returned Results.

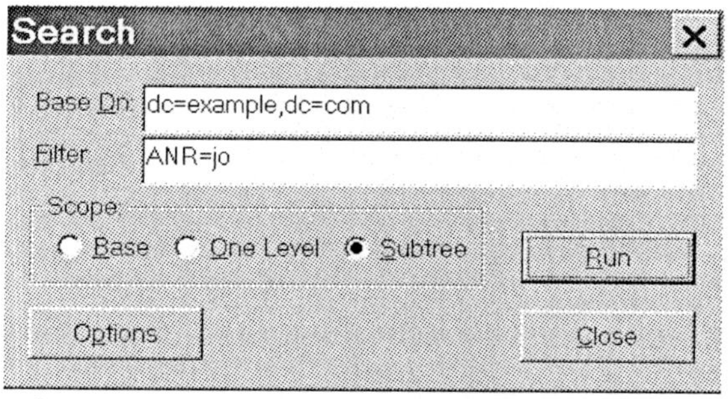

Figure 3.2 – ANR search using LDP

The *searchFlags* property of an attribute specifies whether the attribute is included in ANR searches. The attribute must also be indexed. In Microsoft® Windows® 2000 there are eight attributes that are default members of the ANR set, Microsoft® Windows® Server 2003 adds an additional member to the set. Further attributes can be added to the ANR set using Schema Manager, although you must index them first.

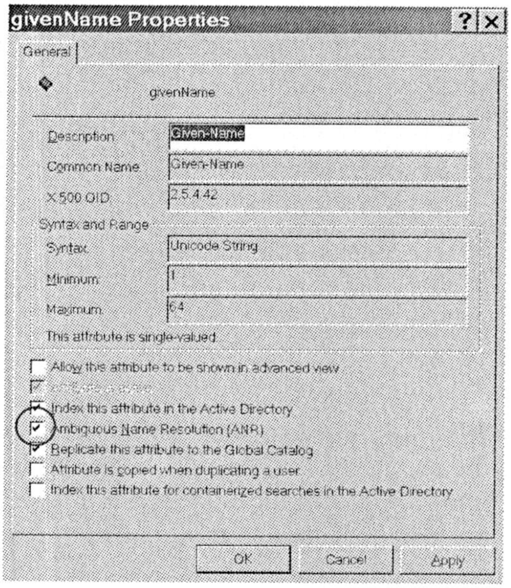

Figure 3.3 –Adding an attribute to the ANR set

ANR – Dual Word Testing

When the input string consists of two words, in addition to testing the input string (with a wildcard appended) against the ANR attribute set, tests are performed using each word of the input string. A test is made to see if the *givenName* attribute value matches the first word AND the *sn* (surname) attribute value matches the second word; if this evaluates TRUE the associated user's name is returned. The test is then reversed and a test is made to see if the *givenName* attribute value matches the second word AND the *sn* (surname) attribute value matches the first word; if this evaluates TRUE the associated user's name is returned.

For example, if you had a user called John Smith you could either search for him by setting the input string to John Smith or Smith John. Alternatively, you could let wildcards do their work and set the search strings to Jo S or Sm J

ANR – dSHeuristics

The value of the *dSHeuristics* attribute of the

cn=directory service,cn=windows nt,cn=services,
cn=configuration,dc=example,dc=com

object controls how the dual word tests are performed.

If the *dSHeuristics* attribute is not set or if the first two characters are 00, the search algorithm as described in Dual Word Testing is performed.

If the first two characters are 10

A test is made to see if the *givenName* attribute value matches the second word AND the *sn* (surname) attribute value matches the first word; if this evaluates TRUE the associated user's name is returned.

If the first two characters are 01

A test is made to see if the *givenName* attribute value matches the first word AND the *sn* (surname) attribute value matches the second word; if this evaluates TRUE the associated user's name is returned.

If the first two characters are 11

The input string is treated as a single word and just tested against the ANR set. For example, the search for Jo S★ would only return a user with Jo S★ as an attribute value of one or more of the members of the ANR set. (ie: *givenName* = Jo Smith or *sn* (surname)=Jo Smith).

Category 1 or 2 Objects and Attributes

Objects and attributes included in the base schema are classified as Category 1. Extensions to the base schema are classified as Category 2.

The *systemFlags* attribute identifies the classification. You can easily set up a search to find all the base schema objects and attributes or extensions by setting a filter that tests the *systemFlags*. See System Flags below and Chapter 6, Advanced Searching with Complex Filters.

The following restrictions apply to any schema objects, category 1 or 2:
  - New attributes cannot be added to the *mustContain* attribute list either directly or through inheritance by adding an auxiliary class
  - Attributes cannot be deleted from the *mustContain* attribute list

There are additional restrictions on category 1 objects. The following attributes cannot be changed:
  - *rangeLower* and *rangeUpper* (value range)
  - *attributeSecurityGUID* (determines which property set the attribute belongs in, if any)
  - *defaultObjectCategory*
  - *objectCategory*
  - *lDAPDisplayName*

In addition you cannot make a category 1 object or attribute definition defunct.

Control Access Rights

Access to Active Directory® objects is controlled via Access Control Lists (ACLs). The ACL may be explicitly set on an object or be inherited. You can use the Access Control Entries (ACEs) to control who can perform standard operations, such as creating and deleting objects, or reading and writing the properties of an object. For some types of *objectClass* you may need to control access in a way that is not supported by the standard access rights that can be applied through ACEs. To support these needs the Active Directory® provides extensions to the standard access control mechanism through *controlAccessRight* objects (be careful not to confuse this with the attribute *controlAccessRights*).

controlAccessRight objects are created in the
cn=extended-rights,cn=configuration...
container and are used to define and control access to property sets, extended rights and validated writes.

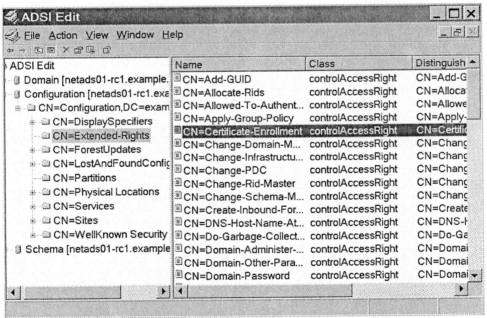

Figure 3.4 – Listing controlAccessRight objects in ADSI Edit

Property sets allow security to be applied to a set of properties through a single ACE entry. The *controlAccessRight* object identifies the members of the property set. As an example, the Personal Information (PI) property set allows a single ACE to control access to 41 individual user properties.

Extended rights provide a mechanism to control access to an operation not covered by the standard access rights. Examples of extended writes are resetting passwords, managing replication and changing FSMO roles.

Validated writes provide a mechanism to control access to write operations that provide validation checking (beyond that provided by the schema) before writing a value to an object's attribute. This ensures that the value conforms to required semantics and other constraints that would not be checked by a normal Directory Service (DS) write. There are three validated writes defined for the Active Directory:

Add/Remove Self as Member
Allows a user to add or remove their own account to or from a group.

Validated Write to DNS Host Name
Allows the DNS host name attribute of a computer object to be set provided the system validates the name.

Validated Write to Service Principal Name
Allows the service principal name attribute of a computer object to be set provided the system validates the name.

New property sets and extended writes can be created but you cannot add additional validated writes as there is no way to change the system to enforce the validation checking.

You can tell whether a *controlAccessRight* object represents a property set, extended right or validated write by the value stored in the object's *validAccesses* attribute.

controlAccessRight	validAccesses attribute value (decimal)
Property set	48
Extended right	256
Validated write	8

The *controlAccessRight* object has an *appliesTo* attribute which is multi-valued and contains the *SchemaIDGUID* for each of the objects that the *controlAccessRight* object is associated with.

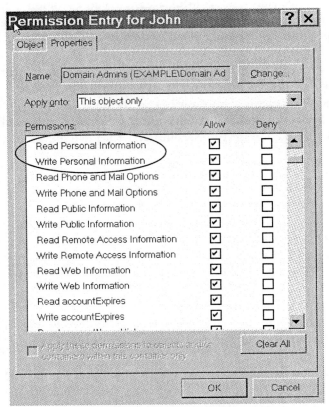

Figure 3.5 – Setting personal information access control

The text string that is used to represent the *controlAccessRight* object in the security user interfaces is held in the object's *displayName* attribute. You will notice in the above figure, the personal information entry. This text string has come from the the *displayName* attribute of the personal information *controlAaccessRight* object.

You may have looked at the security dialogs in the past and wondered why the alphabetical order changes. The list is sorted alphabetically on the second word of the displayed text string. The reason why Read *accountExpires* appears after Write Web Information is because the security on the *controlAccessRight* objects appears in advance of the security on properties.

Creating Objects

When a new object is created in the directory this is referred to as instantiating an instance of an *objectClass*. To create the object the mandatory attributes defined for that object must be populated. Some of these mandatory attributes may be automatically populated by the system; you will have to populate the remaining.

The mandatory attributes are defined as part of the object class definition. These attributes are defined in two multi-valued attributes *systemMustContain* and *mustContain* of the *classSchema* object. If you examined both of these attributes for a user class definition you would find them both empty. Does that mean there are no mandatory attributes required when creating a user object? You can probably answer that for yourself, there are always going to be mandatory attributes for any object you create, as an absolute minimum you will have to supply the name for the object you are creating and also its type.

So where are the mandatory attributes for a user object defined? All classes with the exception of the top class are built from other classes; these are referred to as parent classes. An object class definition identifies its immediate parent by the value held in its *subClassOf* attribute. When you instantiate an object you must populate all of the mandatory attributes defined for the object class and all of the mandatory attributes defined for its parent's class, its grandparent's class, its great grandparent's class and so on.

Let's look at the antecedence of a user class definition:

Class LDAP Display Name	*subClassOf* (parent)	Mandatory attributes *systemMustContain* and *mustContain* values
user	*organizationalPerson*	None
organizationalPerson	*person*	None
person	*top*	*cn*
top	Top-level no parent	*instanceType*, *nTSecurityDescriptor*, *objectClass*, *objectCategory*

In addition to parent classes, object definitions can have auxiliary classes attached. Auxiliary classes have additional attributes which become part of the overall object definition. There are two auxiliary classes attached to the user class definition and these are *securityPrincipal* and *mailRecipient*.

Auxiliary Class	Mandatory attributes *systemMustContain* and *mustContain* values
securityPrincipal	*sAMAccountName, objectSID*
mailRecipient	*cn*

The two tables above demonstrate that it is necessary to populate seven attributes

- *cn*
- *instanceType*
- *nTSecurityDescriptor*
- *objectClass*
- *objectCategory*
- *sAMAccountName*
- *objectSID*

The simplest way of viewing an object's mandatory attributes is to use Schema Manager. Open the classes icon, select the required class (for example user) and all of the attributes are displayed in the results pane. Schema Manager does not display the *classSchema* object and its attributes; it interprets the information and displays all of the attributes that are associated with a particular class. These attributes include the attributes associated with the parent classes; see the section on Schema Manager below for more detail about how the information is displayed.

Selecting the Type column will order the list showing the mandatory and optional attributes. You can see the source class for each of the attributes in the Source Class column. The optional attributes are defined in two multi-valued attributes *systemMayContain* and *mayContain* of the *classSchema* object. As with the mandatory attributes, Schema Manager shows all of the optional attributes that are defined for the actual class definition, the parents and auxiliary classes.

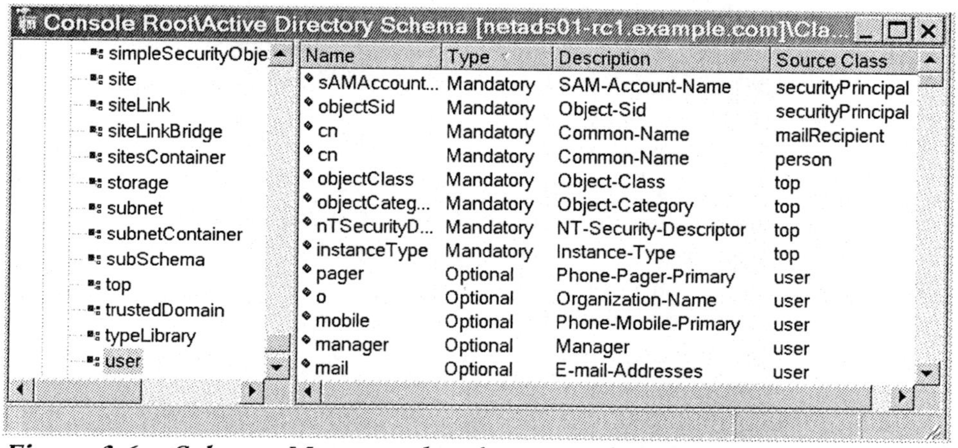

Figure 3.6 – Schema Manager showing user class attributes

So to create a user object the *cn*, *instanceType*, *nTSecurityDescriptor*, *objectClass*, *objectCategory*, *sAMAccountName* and *objectSID* must be populated. In fact the system will automatically populate most of these attributes. As a rule-of-thumb when deciding which attributes you must populate choose the attributes that the system could not generate values for.

In the above list you must specify the name (*cn*), the type of object you are creating (*objectClass*) and the SAM account name (*sAMAccountName*). The system will automatically fill in the rest. Microsoft® Windows® Server 2003 goes one step further and automatically generates a SAM account name if you don't supply one. In reality when you create a user account you will want to specify more attribute values, including the user principal name and account control settings.

For details of creating users with LDP see Chapter 8, Manipulating Objects and Attributes.

Deleted Objects

When an object is deleted, most of its attributes are stripped (for details of which attributes are retained see the *searchFlags* earlier in this chapter), the *isDeleted* attribute is set TRUE and the object is moved to the Deleted Objects container. The object is said to be tombstoned.

The object is retained in the directory for a default tombstone life of 60 days. The object remains in the directory so that the fact that it has been deleted can be replicated to all appropriate domain controllers. Once the tombstone period expires, the garbage collection service will purge the object from the directory. Backups older that the tombstone period cannot be used as they could unintentionally restore deleted objects.

A standard LDAP search will not return objects in the Deleted Objects container. To retrieve these objects you need to use an LDAP control. See examples in Chapter 7, Controlling Returned Results.

Display Specifiers

Object classes are defined in the schema using a *classSchema* object. In addition to the formal definition of the object class a display specifier can be defined that specifies the user interface configuration for that class. For example the user class display specifier defines the property sheets, context menus, icons and creation wizards. The Microsoft® Windows® shell and Active Directory® administrative snap-ins use this information to define different interfaces for administrators and users.

Localization is supported through the definition of display specifiers for each of the supported locales. The display specifier objects for each locale are stored in a locale-specific container within the cn=DisplaySpecifiers,cn=configuration... container.

The language identifier is used as the name for the locale-specific container, for example 409 is the language identifier for US-English and 409 is used as the name for the locale-specific container.

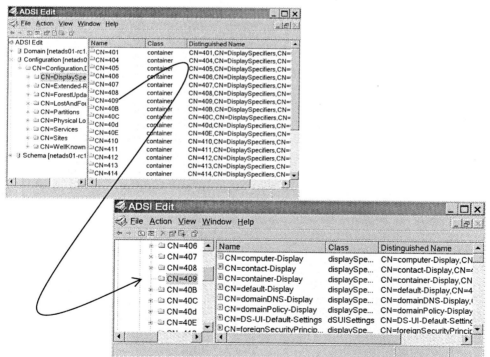

Figure 3.7 – Display specifier locales

The individual display specifiers are named after the object class with which they are associated. The user display specifier is identified by cn=user-Display, the one for a computer object is cn=computer-Display and so on.

The display specifier also defines the relationship between the text strings used to identify the attribute values displayed in the user interface and the LDAP display names of the attributes that store data. This relationship is defined in the multi-valued *attributeDisplayNames* attribute.

For example if you open the properties dialog for a user object and select the Telephones tab, you will see that you can enter a value for a Fax number.

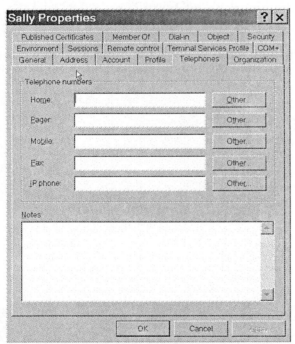

Figure 3.8 – Telephones property page

Examine the *attributeDisplayNames* attribute for the appropriate locale to find the name of the attribute that stores the number.

The UI to LDAP display name mappings for a US-English (409) user object are shown in Appendix B.

A locale table can be found in Appendix F.

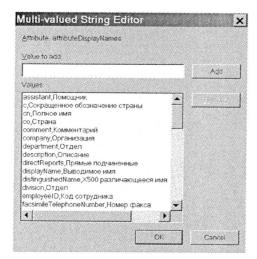

419, Russian: Russia

403, Dutch: Netherlands

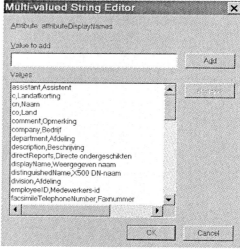

Figure 3.9 – Attribute display names

409, English: United States

Figure 3.10 – Attribute display names for locale 409

In the display specifier for the 409 locale, you can see the following entry:

---

facsimileTelephoneNumber,Fax Number

So now you know that the fax number is stored in an attribute called *facsimileTelephoneNumber*. OK, if you have been very observant you will have noticed that the user interface field used the name Fax and the display specifier showed Fax Number.

So here's the caveat. Most of the UI strings are hard coded, however the strings used are very similar and it is normally possible to identify the attribute associated with the UI text string.

Whenever attributes are displayed in the security dialogs the *attributeDisplayNames* mappings are used. When it comes to defining security on the user's fax number you will see the appropriate string appear in the dialog. If you edit the display specifier text value this new text will appear. To see the changes in Active Directory® Users and Computers you will need to restart it.

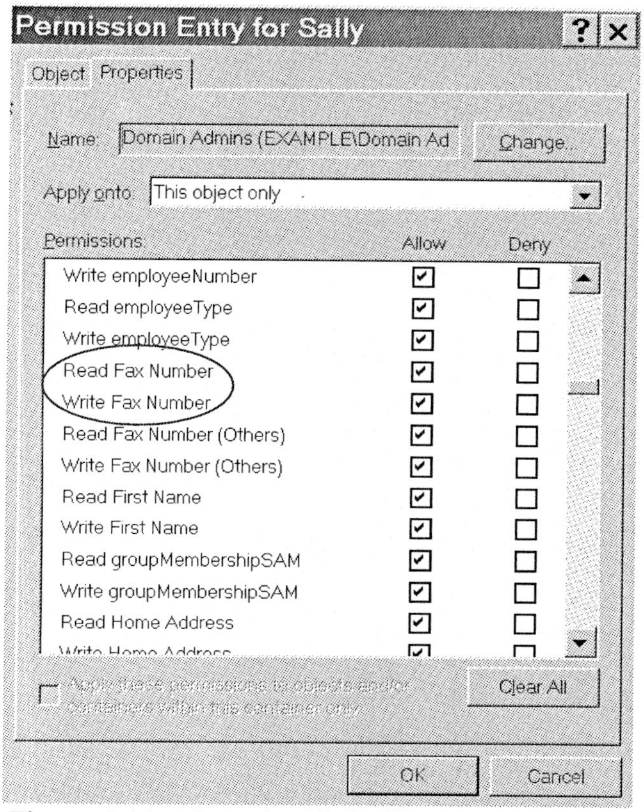

Figure 3.11 – Security dialog showing fax number

The display specifiers are loaded into the directory when the first domain controller is created in a new forest. They are loaded from a clear text file called dcpromo.csv. This file is in Comma Separated Value (CSV) format. During the first logon after the promotion of the domain controller using dcpromo.exe, dchelp.exe executes and loads the display specifiers. It uses csvde.exe to import the file.

Global Catalog

Forest-wide searches are directed at the global catalog (GC). A global catalog always runs on a domain controller and maintains a directory database of all the objects in the forest, it will respond to LDAP queries on port 3268. In a single domain environment the directory database on a domain controller already contains all of the objects from the forest. Consequently specifying the server to also be a GC involves no additional replication.

In a multi-domain environment a GC in one domain will have to "pull" all the objects from domain controllers in the other domains. Replication is minimized by limiting the number of attributes that are replicated to the GC. The attributes that are replicated are referred to as the Partial Attribute Set (PAS).

Attributes that are members of the PAS have their *isMemberOfPartialAttributeSet* property set TRUE. This property can be changed via Schema Manager.

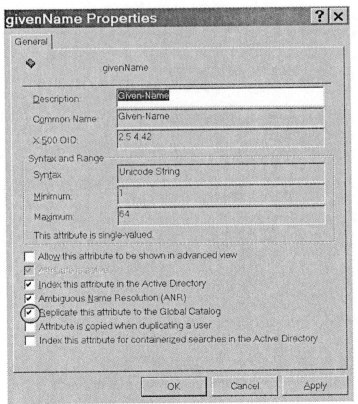

Figure 3.12 – Adding an attribute to the PAS

There is a caveat to adding an attribute to the PAS. It causes all of the GCs to fully resynchronise. In a single domain environment, this does not have an impact as the DCs already have the GC information. In a multi-domain environment, resynchronisation causes significant network traffic as all the objects have to be pulled into the GCs again.

There are replication improvements in Microsoft® Windows® Server 2003. When the forest is running at .NET forest functionality level, adding to the PAS does not cause full GC resynchronisation, only the added attributes are replicated.

Groups

The Active Directory® supports a number of different groups; these are specified by scope (Domain Local, Global or Universal) and type (security or distribution). All groups are defined using a single class called *group* and the *groupType* property identifies the group's scope and type. The *groupType* is an integer value with individual bits identifying the group characteristics:

Bit	Value	Description of attribute properties
1	2	Set for global groups
2	4	Set for domain local groups
4	8	Set for universal groups
31	2147483648	Set for security groups, clear for distribution groups

To test the group types you will need to use matching rules. See Matching Rules in this chapter. For examples, see Chapter 6, Advanced Searching with Complex Filters.

Universal security groups only exist for native mode domains, the *nTMixedDomain* property of the *domainDNS* object for the domain identifies the operating mode. This is an integer value which is 0 (zero) for native mode and 1 (one) or not set for mixed.

GUIDs

Globally Unique Identifiers (GUIDs) are 128 bit numbers that can be used to uniquely identify objects and other entities. If an object is moved, its DN always changes but the GUID remains the same. This applies even for cross-domain moves.

You can generate a GUID using the Software Development Kit (SDK) utilities guidgen.exe or uuidgen.exe. UUID stands for Universally Unique Identifier and can be used interchangeable with GUID.

An object's GUID is stored in the *objectGUID* attribute.

If you know the GUID of an object you can always locate it. You can also define the base for a LDAP search using the base object's GUID rather than its DN. See Chapter 5, Getting to Grips with Searching.

GUIDs are stored in the directory in either GUID string or binary octet string format.

GUID string	7147a8de-129a-4edd-9533-83982050211f
Binary octet string	de a8 47 71 9a 12 dd 4e 95 33 83 98 20 50 21 1f

These two values actually represent the same GUID! In certain situations you will need to convert between them.

LDP converts and displays GUIDs stored in octet format into the GUID string format. If you want to display the GUID in hex you need to set the LDP option **Value Parsing** to binary. You will find this option in the General Options dialog, invoke the dialog via **Options | General**.

Each pair of digits in the binary octet string is written in hexadecimal and represents a byte. The GUID string is also written in hexadecimal bytes in the format: 4 bytes − 2 bytes − 2 bytes − 2 bytes − 6 bytes. Apart from the character spacing and dashes the only difference between the octet string and GUID string formats is that the bytes are written in reverse order for each of the first three numeric sequences.

Converting GUID string to octet string

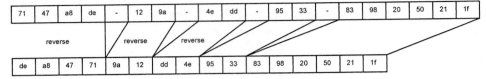

Figure 3.13 – Converting GUID string to octet string

You have to be careful of these different formats when using LDP. As an example, if you retrieve the *attributeSecurityGUID* of an attribute using LDP it will display it as a GUID string, as follows:

```
Getting 1 entries:
>> Dn:
CN=Description,CN=Schema,CN=Configuration,DC=example,DC=com
attributeSecurityGUID: e48d0154-bcf8-11d1-8702-00c04fb96050;
```

In fact, this value is stored in the directory in binary octet string format and LDP has converted it to GUID string format when it displays the returned value.

If you wanted to search for an *attributeSecurityGUID* set to the above value, a search using the GUID string will fail.

For example, the following will not work
(attributeSecurityGUID=e48d0154-bcf8-11d1-8702-00c04fb96050)

You need to search using the binary octet string.

Convert the value to octet format:
54 01 8d e4 f8 bc d1 11 87 02 00 c0 4f b9 60 50

To search for a GUID string in octet format using LDP requires each byte to be preceded by a backslash escape character "\".

The test should be:
(attributeSecurityGUID=\54\01\8d\e4\f8\bc\d1\11\87\02\00\c0\4f\b9\60\50)

Indexed Attributes

Indexing attributes that are used in directory searches will enhance performance. Values used when querying indexed attributes should be restricted to exact matches or substrings starting with the word fragment and ending in a wildcard (nam*).

Microsoft® Windows® Server 2003 includes the ability to set medial indexes, which support queries where the wildcard appears first (*ame).

Identify/set indexed attributes via their *searchFlags* property. The flag can be viewed through Schema Manager.

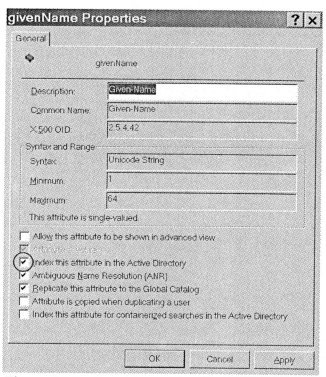

Figure 3.14 – Indexing an attribute

You can see which indexes are being used in a search by enabling the Search Stats LDAP control. See Chapter 7, Controlling Returned Results.

LDAP Controls

LDAP controls extend the server or client LDAP functionality. The server can be instructed to respond differently by sending an extended LDAP command with an attached control.

The controls that are supported can be enumerated through RootDSE and are identified by OIDs.

You can use controls with LDP, some of the more useful ones are listed below.

Control OID	Requests the server to...
1.2.840.113556.1.4.805	Allow subtree delete. (including deletion of contained objects.)
1.2.840.113556.1.4.417	Return deleted (tombstoned) objects.
1.2.840.113556.1.4.473	Sort the results. This is set in LDP through the Sort Keys option.
2.16.840.1.113730.3.4.9	Enable Virtual List View (VLV) support. Only available on Microsoft® Windows® Server 2003.
1.2.840.113556.1.4.970	Requests the server to return statistics on how the LDAP operation was performed.

To see how controls are set, see Chapter 7, Controlling Returned Results.

LDAP Display Names

Whenever an attribute is referenced in an LDAP operation or programmatically through Active Directory® Service Interfaces (ADSI), the attribute's LDAP display name must be used. The LDAP display name is defined in an attribute's *lDAPDisplayName* property as part of the schema definition of the attribute. The Common Name (*cn*) of the attribute and the LDAP display name may be different. You can map between the names using LDP, ADSI Edit or Schema Manager. See below and Appendix C and D.

When you view the schema using ADSI Edit, the object and attribute definitions are identified by common name.

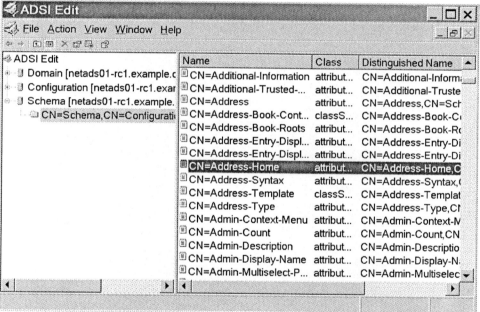

Figure 3.15 – ADSI Edit sorting by common name

To retrieve the LDAP display name, examine the properties of the object or attribute and view the value for the *lDAPdisplayName* property.

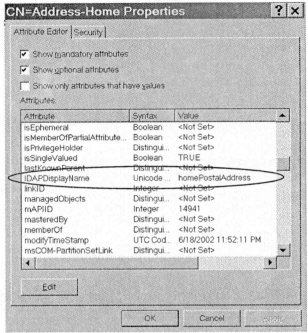

Figure 3.16 – Retrieving the LDAP display name

Schema Manager identifies objects (classes) and attributes by their LDAP display name.

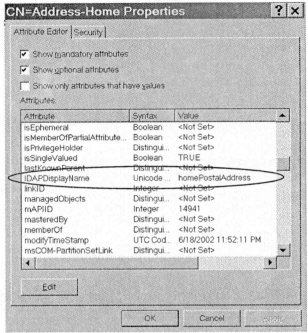

Figure 3.17 – Schema Manager sorting by LDAP display name

To retrieve the common name of an object or attribute, view the associated property dialog (the common name is sometimes listed as the description in the Description column).

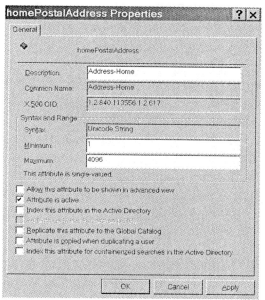

Figure 3.18 – homePostalAddress properties

When you are viewing an object through the user interface using tools such as Active Directory® Users and Computers, the different fields shown in dialogs relate to values stored in attributes. Each object has an associated display specifier which defines the relationship between the name used to identify the field in the user interface and the LDAP display name of the attribute in which the data is stored. The UI to LDAP display name mappings for user object are shown in Appendix B. See Display Specifiers above for more details.

LDAP Policies

LDAP policies define operational parameters for the LDAP service on a domain controller. These policies can be viewed and set via the command line tool ntdsutil.exe:

```
C:\>ntdsutil
ntdsutil: ldap policies
ldap policy: connections
server connections: connect to server netads01-rc1...
Binding to netads01-rc1...
Connected to netads01-rc1... using credentials of
locally logged on user
server connections: q
ldap policy: show values

Policy                    Current(New)

MaxPoolThreads            4
MaxDatagramRecv           1024
MaxReceiveBuffer          10485760
InitRecvTimeout           120
MaxConnections            5000
MaxConnIdleTime           900
MaxActiveQueries          20
MaxPageSize               1000
MaxQueryDuration          120
MaxTempTableSize          10000
MaxResultSetSize          262144
MaxNotificationPerConn    5

ldap policy: q
ntdsutil: q
Disconnecting from netads01-rc1 ...
```

The policies are set to limit the impact of LDAP operation on the server's overall performance and provide resilience against denial of service attacks.

The following list explains each policy. You will see that the MaxPageSize defaults to 1000 records. This defines the maximum number of records that can be returned from the server in any one query. If the results set you are requesting is greater than 1000 records it is possible to modify this value and return more records. For large sets of results it is better to page the returned results or if you are running Microsoft® Windows® Server 2003 use Virtual List View (VLV). See Chapter 7, Controlling Returned Results.

LDAP Policy	Description	Default Value
MaxPoolThreads	Maximum number of threads per processor that are created for queries.	4
MaxDatagramRecv	Maximum size of a datagram that can be received by a server.	1024 bytes (Windows 2000) 4096 bytes (Server 2003)
MaxReceiveBuffer	Maximum size of LDAP request.	10,485,760 bytes
InitRecvTimeout	If the connection remains idle for more than this time after the initial request. The server drops the connection.	120 seconds
MaxConnections	The maximum number of open LDAP connections that the server will support.	5000
MaxConnIdleTime	If the connection remains idle for more than this time. The server drops the connection.	900 seconds
MaxActiveQueries Not exposed on Microsoft® Windows® Server 2003 (RC1)	If the number of concurrent searches exceeds this value, the LDAP server returns a busy notification	20
MaxPageSize	Maximum number of records that a server will return.	1000
MaxQueryDuration	Maximum time allowed for a query to complete. If the time is exceeded the server returns a timeLimitExceeded error	120 seconds

LDAP Policy	Description	Default Value
MaxTempTableSize	Maximum size of temporary storage allocated for the execution of queries	10,000
MaximumResultSetSize	The maximum storage that is allocated to hold paged result sets. If this is exhausted the oldest result sets are discarded	262,144 bytes
MaxNotificationsPer Connection	Maximum number of notification requests per connection. If this value is exceeded, the LDAP server returns a busy notification.	5

LDAP Synchronous versus Asynchronous Operations

Most LDAP function calls have both synchronous and asynchronous versions. The synchronous versions have a **_s** suffix appended to the function call name and you can see these in LDP. For example **ldap_search_s** is a synchronous search.

Synchronous function calls must return before the client can continue. Asynchronous function calls allow the client to continue with other tasks while the request is being processed. The client can even submit further LDAP requests while a previous asynchronous request is being processed. A message identifier identifies each request and the client can ask the server to return the status of the call using the identifier.

All our examples in this book use synchronous requests. Using LDP it is possible to generate asynchronous requests by selecting the appropriate check boxes in the Search Options dialog page. You can then retrieve the results using **Browse | Process Pending**.

Linked Attributes

Pairs of attributes can be linked. A forward-link attribute on a source object references a target object by its distinguished name (*dn*). The back-link attribute on the target object is automatically calculated and populated with the DN of the source object.

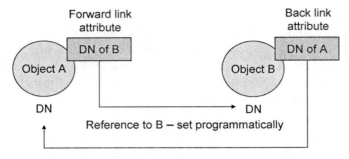

Figure 3.19 – Linked attributes

For example, a user object has both a *manager* and *directReports* attribute and these are linked. When a user's *manager* attribute is set to the DN of the manager, the manager's *directReports* attribute is automatically calculated and populated with the DN of the user. In the properties dialog for a user account object, the fields that populate the *manager* and *directReports* attributes are on the Organization property sheet. The Direct Reports field cannot be manually edited.

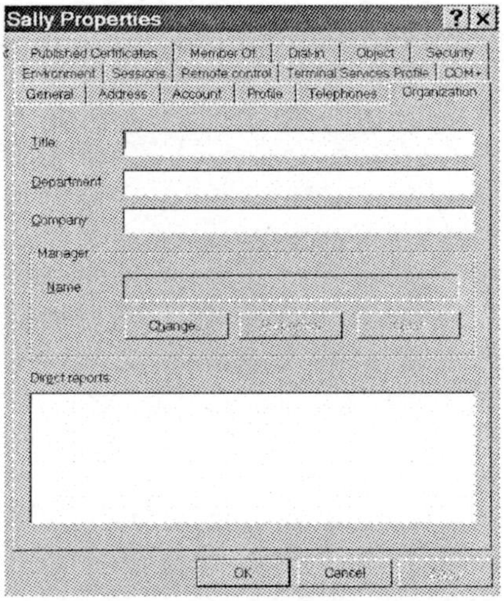

Figure 3.20 – Organizational properties

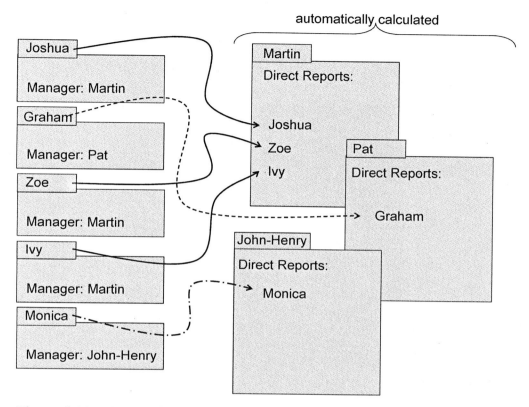

Figure 3.20 – Forward-links and back-links

Forward-link and back-link pairs are identified by their *linkID* property values. A forward-link has the *linkID* set to an even number (*n*) and the associated back-link has its *linkID* property value set to n+1 (always odd). For instance the *linkID* property of the *manager* attribute is set to 42 and the *linkID* property of the *directReports* attribute is set to 43.

The following rules apply to linked attributes:
  -   The *linkID* values must be unique for linked pairs. If you are planning to create new linked pairs Microsoft will supply, via their website, a range of *linkID* values that will be unique for your organization
  -   Back links are always multi-valued
  -   Forward links can be single or multi-valued
  -   Multi-valued forward links are used for many-to-many relationships

The *member* and *memberOf* attributes are an example of a many-to-many relationship. The *member* attribute (*linkID*=2) value lists the members of a group and the *memberOf* attribute (*linkID*=3) lists a user's membership of groups. See Chapter 7, Sort Keys for usage on enumerating linked attributes and sorting them.

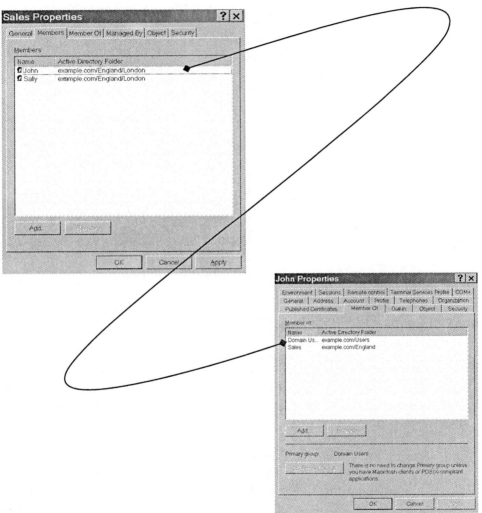

Figure 3.21 – Group membership linked attributes

Matching Rules

A matching rule specifies how attribute values are to be matched for equality, ordering and substring comparison. Microsoft defines two rules that can be used for bitwise testing.

The least significant bit within a numeric value is referred to as bit 0, the next bit 1 and so on.

Bit to test	Bit 7	Bit 6	Bit 5	Bit 4	Bit 3	Bit 2	Bit 1	Bit 0
Binary value	128	64	32	16	8	4	2	1

Some attributes in the Active Directory® are composed of bitwise flags. For instance bit 0 of the *searchFlags* property of an attribute defines if the attribute is indexed. Bit 1 defines if the attribute is indexed for containerized searches and bit 2 defines if the attribute is included in ANR searches. Other bits of the *searchFlags* property define other behaviours.

Test to see if an attribute is indexed by testing the value of an individual bit within the *searchFlags*. It is no good testing the numeric value of the flags.

As an example, if an attribute is indexed, bit 0 of the *searchFlags* will be set. If this is the only flag set, the *searchFlags* would have a numeric value of 1. However if the attribute was also included in ANR searches bit 2 would be set. This means the flags would have a numeric value of 5 (1 + 4).

So should we test for a value of 1 or 5 if we want to know if the attribute is indexed?

Neither, you need to test individual bits within an attribute and this requires a bitwise operation.

The bitwise tests can be defined in LDAP filters and are in the following format (notice the colons and no spaces):

Attributename:RuleOID:=Value

Attributename is the attribute to be tested. In our example above this would be the *searchFlags*. The **RuleOID** defines an AND or an OR bit test and **Value** is the numeric value in decimal of all the bits that should be included in the test. The value is calculated by adding up the binary values of each of the bits to be tested.

- An AND test will evaluate TRUE if ALL of the bits identified by the numeric value are set
- An OR test will evaluate TRUE if ANY of the bits identified by the numeric value are set

RuleOID
  1.2.840.113556.1.4.803 defines an AND test
  1.2.840.113556.1.4.804 defines an OR test

To test if an attribute is indexed, test its *searchFlags* property (defined in the schema) using the following matching rule:

searchFlags:1.2.840.113556.1.4.803:=1

To test if an attribute is indexed and included in ANR searches use:

searchFlags:1.2.840.113556.1.4.803:=5

Object Names

Each object has a Relative Distinguished Name (RDN) and this name must be unique within any container. The Distinguished Name (DN) of the object is a concatenation of the object's RDN and the RDNs for each of the nodes in the objects path. The DN must be unique in the forest.

The attribute that holds the RDN for a particular object class is identified by the *rDNAttID* attribute. In most cases the *rDNAttID* specifies the common name (*cn*) attribute to hold an object's RDN.

- For an Organization-Unit object the *ou* attribute holds the RDN
- For a Domain-DNS object the *dc* attribute holds the RDN

A successful LDAP query always returns the DN of the object together with the specified attributes.

You can use the **Modify RDN** dialog in LDP to change the DN of the object. If you change the object's path this will have the effect of moving the object. See Chapter 8, Manipulating Objects and Attributes.

Object Class and Object Category

Object instances in the directory have a multi-valued *objectClass* attribute. This attribute identifies the class of the particular object as well as all its parent classes. For instance the *objectClass* attribute value for a user account object will be set to: *user, organizationalPerson, person* and *top*. The *objectClass* attribute does not identify the object's auxiliary classes. The *objectClass* attribute is set by the system when the object is created and cannot be changed.

If you search using an *objectClass* filter for example (objectClass=user), there are a couple of disadvantages. Firstly the *objectClass* attribute is not indexed so searches are not optimal. Don't decide to index the attribute, it is multi-valued and all definitions will contain the *top* class which would make the index very large and inefficient. The second caveat to searching is that as the attribute is multi-valued you will return all instances where the attribute contains your search value. The parent class for a computer object is *user*, consequently the *objectClass* attribute for a computer object will contain: *computer, user, organizationalPerson, person* and *top*. A search for (objectClass=user) will also evaluate TRUE for computer objects as well as user objects.

To simplify searching, in addition to the *objectClass* attribute, each object also has an *objectCategory* attribute. This attribute is single-valued, indexed and contains the distinguished name of either the object's class or one of its parent classes. When an object is created, the *objectCategory* value is set to the value contained in the *defaultObjectCategory* attribute which is defined in the schema as part of the class definition. When an object is created the *objectCategory* value is set by the system and cannot be changed.

Most object definitions have their *defaultObjectCategory* attributes set to the same name as the DN for the class. However it is possible for the *defaultObjectCategory* attribute to refer to another class, this simplifies searching for a group of related classes. As an example the *defaultObjectCategory* attribute for the object definitions of *user, contact, organizationalPerson, person* and *inetOrgPerson* are all set to the same DN:

> cn=person,cn=schema, cn=configuration,<dc=forestroot>

Consequently you can find all "people" in the directory with a single search filter:

> (objectCategory=cn=person,cn=schema,cn=configuration,<dc=forestroot>)

When using the *objectCategory* attribute you could specify the appropriate DN. As an alternative to the DN, it is possible to use the LDAP display name of the *objectClass*. The server looks up the associated *objectCategory* DN before constructing the filter.

As an example if you set the filter to:

(objectCategory=user) or (objectCategory=contact)

The server expands the filter to:

(objectCategory=cn=person,cn=schema,cn=configuration,<dc=forestroot>)

If you set the filter to:

(objectCategory=organizationalUnit)

The server expands the filter to:

(objectCategory=cn=organizational-unit,cn=schema,cn=configuration,<dc=forestroot>)

You can observe the filter expansion if you use the Search Stats control. See Returning Search Statistics in Chapter 7.

OIDs.

Object Identifiers (OIDs) provide a unique and universal way to reference an object. Here an object does not just mean an Active Directory® object, it refers to a "thing". The thing might be an object definition, attribute definition, syntax and so on. The Abstract Syntax Notation One (ANS.1) standard defines an object as *"a well-defined piece of information, definition or specification…"*

An OID is a unique identifier within a hierarchal name space. The OID is written as a string of numbers with each number separated by a dot (1.2.840.113556). An authority (organization) is allocated a base OID and they can allocate any number of OIDs below that base. For instance 1.2.840.113556 is a base OID that has been allocated to Microsoft. Consequently Microsoft can assign all extensions to the base, such as 1.2.840.113556.1, 1.2.840.113556.2 etc. This is similar to the Internet DNS name space where an organization is allocated a DNS name and then they can allocate any number of additional subdomains.

Base OID	Authority
1	ISO
1.2	ANSI
1.2.840	USA
1.2.840.113556	Microsoft
1.2.840.113556.1	Microsoft: used for Active Directory®

If you are going to be creating schema extensions and commercially distributing these with an application, then it would be wise to obtain a base OID which is registered with ISO. There is normally a fee associated with this. Alternatively you can use the Resource Kit utility oidgen.exe to generate a base OID or you could obtain an OID from Microsoft via their website. Both of these last two options will provide you with an OID which is subordinate to the Microsoft 1.2.840.113556 base OID.

If you are making schema changes you will have to define LDAP display names, common names etc. You should register a name prefix with Microsoft. This prefix is used as the stem for all of your schema extension names. In addition to providing prefix registration and OID generation, Microsoft will also supply a range of *linkID* attribute values that will be unique to your organization.

Operational Attributes

Operational attributes are attributes that are used for administration purposes. These attributes are not defined in the schema and do not take up any storage. When an operational attribute is read, if it returns a value, the value is calculated by the server. Writing to an operational attribute triggers an action on the server.

Operational attributes are defined in RFC 2252.

The operational attributes that can be read are the RootDSE attributes, for example:

- *namingContexts*
- *defaultNamingContext*
- *schemaNamingContext*
- *configurationNamingContext*
- *rootDomainNamingContext*
- *supportedControl*
- *supportedLDAPVersion*

Examples of operational attributes that can be written:

schemaUpdateNow	Updates the in-memory schema cache
updateCachedMemberships	Updates the universal group caches on a domain controller. Only used with Microsoft® Windows® Server 2003 2003
becomeRidMaster	Transfers the RID master role
becomeSchemaMaster	Transfers the schema master role

Property Sets

Property sets allow security to be applied through a single ACE entry. The *controlAccessRight* object identifies the members of the property set. As an example the Personal Information (PI) property set allows a single ACE to control access to 41 individual user properties.

Property sets can apply to one or more objects. The objects with which the property set can be used are identified by the *appliesTo* attribute of the *controlAccessRight* object. This attribute is multi-valued and holds the *schemaIDGUID* value for each of the objects that are associated with the property set.

Using ADSI Edit you can see that the Personal Information property set can be used with the following objects:

- — *inetOrgPerson*
- — *contact*
- — *computer*
- — *user*

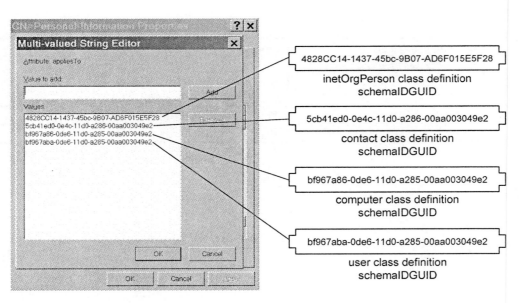

Figure 3.22 – appliesTo attribute

The attributes that belong to a property set are identified by another GUID. This GUID value is stored in the *rightsGuid* attribute of the *controlAccessRight* object that defines the property set and also in the *attributeSecurityGUID* property of each attribute that is a member of the property set.

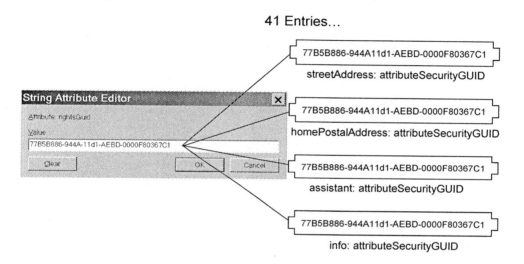

41 Entries...

77B5B886-944A11d1-AEBD-0000F80367C1
streetAddress: attributeSecurityGUID

77B5B886-944A11d1-AEBD-0000F80367C1
homePostalAddress: attributeSecurityGUID

77B5B886-944A11d1-AEBD-0000F80367C1
assistant: attributeSecurityGUID

77B5B886-944A11d1-AEBD-0000F80367C1
info: attributeSecurityGUID

Figure 3.23 - rightsGuid attribute

So you might be thinking that all you have to do to identify all members of a property set is to retrieve the *rightsGuid* value from the appropriate *controlAccessRight* object and search for all attributes which have an *attributeSecurityGUID* matching this value. Unfortunately life is never that simple! The *rightsGuid* is stored in GUID string format and the *attributeSecurityGUID* is stored as a binary octet string. Before you can run the search you will need to convert the GUID string to an octet string, see the entry for GUIDs in this chapter.

RootDSE

RootDSE (DSA-Specific Entry) is defined for LDAP v3.0 as the root of the Directory Information Tree (DIT) on a directory server. RootDSE is accessible on any directory server and provides forest and domain information about the directory. RootDSE is not part of any naming context and can be retrieved without the need to supply any credentials.

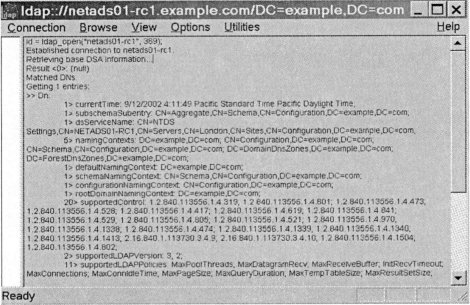

Figure 3.24 – RootDSE

RootDSE is defined in RFCs 2251 and 2252. These definitions require a Directory System Agent (DSA), which is a domain controller in the Active Directory®, to provide seven pieces of mandatory information.

In addition to the mandatory requirements, a Microsoft® Windows® 2000 or Server 2003™ domain controller returns additional system information.

Through RootDSE you can retrieve information on the naming contexts supported on the server, LDAP controls, supported policies and much more. For details of all the entries returned see Chapter 4, LDP Primer.

Replicated Attributes

The majority of attribute values in the Active Directory® will be replicated. There are some attributes where the values are kept local to a domain controller and these are not replicated. The *systemFlags* property of an attribute definition in the schema identifies if it should be replicated or not.

Microsoft® Windows® 2000 replicates changes at attribute level. If an attribute changes the contents of the attribute is replicated in its entirety. This type of replication applies to all attributes including ones that hold multiple values. For example, group membership is held in the multi-valued *member* attribute and if one member of a group changes the entire group membership is replicated.

The fact that multi-valued attributes are replicated in their entirety imposes a recommended maximum 5000 group membership limit. This is not a hard limit but a limit set by testing. The issue surrounds transactional updates to the directory; an attribute change must either be committed or rolled back. Active Directory® must hold a temporary copy of the attribute being changed in its version store. The version store is a finite resource and with large transactions (large group membership) there is a possibility of the resource being exhausted. To avoid this situation a maximum group membership size of under 5000 is recommended.

Microsoft® Windows® Server 2003 includes Linked Value Replication (LVR) which allows individual group membership changes to be replicated rather than the complete attribute. This eliminates the 5000 group membership limit and significantly reduces replication traffic. In order to use linked value replication Microsoft® Windows® Server 2003 must be running at .NET forest functionality level.

Schema Manager

Schema Manager is supplied as an MMC snap-in but cannot be installed until the associated DLL is registered. The DLL is automatically registered when the Admin Pack is installed; alternatively it can be registered by running "regsvr32 schmmgmt" at a command prompt.

Despite its name, Schema Manager does not give you a direct view of the schema definition of an object. Each object class definition in the schema defines must-have and may-have attributes along with the parent class from which it is derived. If you examine the schema with ADSI Edit you will see these individual class definitions. When viewing an object class definition through Schema Manager you will see all of the attributes that must (mandatory) and may (optional) be populated when you create an instance of that class in the directory. The mandatory and optional attributes are an aggregation of all of the attributes associated with the object class definition combined with its parent, grandparent, great grandparent... definitions.

See Chapter 8, Manipulating Objects and Attributes.

Searches

A standard search of the directory will be looking for a match between the data held in the directory and the criteria specified in the search filter. The search filter may specify a single attribute and value such as:

(givenName=john)

or a more complex expression using logical operators such as:

(&(givenName=john)(sn=craddock))

In addition to setting the search filter you will need to specify the start point for the search. The search will always start at an object and provided it's not a leaf object it can propagate down through the appropriate subtree. The start point can be specified by the DN, GUID or SID (for security principals) of the selected object.

The scope (depth) of the search can be specified as base, one level, or subtree.

For examples and usage see Chapter 5, Getting to Grips with Searching and Chapter 6, Advanced Searching with Complex Filters.

Search Flags

Attributes defined in the schema can have a *searchFlags* property. The *searchFlags* property holds an integer value and individual bits define different characteristics for the attribute. You can create filters to test these bits using matching rules. See Matching Rules in this chapter.

Bit	Value	Description of the Attribute Property
0	1	Index the attribute
1	2	Index each container that holds an object that uses the attribute
2	4	Include the attribute in ANR searches (must also be indexed)
3	8	Preserve attribute on logical deletion
4	16	Copy the attribute value when a user object is copied
5	32	Index the attribute for medial searches (Only supported on Microsoft® Windows® Server 2003)

SIDs and RIDs

Users, computers and groups are known as security principals and identified by a Security Identifier (SID). Each SID is constructed from a domain-wide SID concatenated with a monotonically-increasing Relative Identifier (RID). The RIDs are allocated by the domain controllers within a domain. To ensure that SIDs are unique, each domain controller is assigned a pool of RIDs by the RID Master. As the pool is depleted the domain controller can apply to the RID Master for another pool. The RID Master allocates 500 RIDs at a time and guarantees that the assigned pools do not overlap.

See SIDs and RIDs in Chapter 5.

System Flags

Objects and attributes can have a *systemFlags* property (attribute). The *systemFlags* hold an integer value and individual bits define different properties for the object or attribute. You can create filters to test these bits using matching rules.

The most important properties defined by *systemFlags* are shown below. Other bits identify whether an object can be moved or deleted and the type of naming context and so on.

Bit	Value	Description of Attribute Properties
0	1	If this bit is set in the *systemFlags* property of an attribute, the attribute is not to be replicated.
2	4	If this bit is set in the *systemFlags* property of an attribute, the attribute is constructed.
4	16	Set for Category 1 objects and attributes, 0/not set for Category 2

To test these flags see Matching Rules. For examples of enumerating Category 1 and Category 2, see Chapter 6, Advanced Searching with Complex Filters.

Timeouts

If you make an LDAP request to a server that you know is heavily loaded it may be desirable to restrict the search time on the server. The time limit can be specified in the API call. This will stop your query from hogging the system. If it times out you can run the query again when the server is less busy.

There is an LDAP policy that restricts the time that a server can spend executing a query. This value will always restrict the maximum time limit regardless of the time that is specified in the LDAP request. See LDAP policies above.

If a timeout is not specified in the LDAP request, the default is assumed to be "no limit".

A client can also specify how long it is prepared to wait for the server to return the results set. If the server fails to respond in this time, the client will abandon the request. We recommend when using LDP to set the timeout value to 120s. This is the server side timeout on any query set by the LDAP policy on the server. If you are writing an application to query the directory you would want to restrict this time so the client doesn't hang around too long!

You can set time limits in LDP via the Search Options dialog.

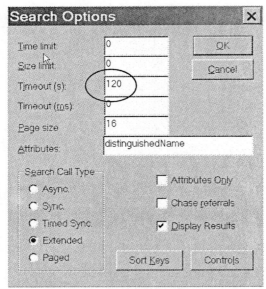

Figure 3.25 – LDP search parameters

Time limit (maximum constrained by the server policy) is a value sent to the server and it instructs the server to abandon the search after this time. The server will return what results it has.

Size limit (maximum constrained by the server policy) is a value sent to the server and instructs the server only to return the defined number of records.

Timeout is the client side time out and only applies to Timed Sync, Extended and Paged search call types. For other calls it is unlimited. If the client does not have a reply within this time it sends an LDAP abandon request. Increase the timeout in seconds if you ever see LDP responding as follows:

```
Error: Search: Timeout. <85>
Error<94>: ldap_parse_result failed: No result present in message
Getting 0 entries:
```

Virtual List View (VLV)

Virtual list view is only available on Microsoft® Windows® Server 2003.

VLV provides a mechanism to retrieve a portion of the results. The results are displayed in a list window and from a user's perspective it appears as though you are simply scrolling through the results. In actual operation the client requests information from the server when required.

The results are alphabetically sorted and the server returns a portion of these results to fill the list view. The results returned are either based on an offset (scrollbar position) into the overall result set or are relative to a selected value for the sorted attribute.

See Chapter 7 for examples of using VLV.

Chapter 4 – LDP Primer

LDP is a generic tool that can be used to interrogate any LDAP directory. We are focusing on interacting with Microsoft® Windows® Active Directory® and will only provide a cursory mention of features that are not directly applicable to Active Directory®.

Some features that we will be covering are only available on Microsoft® Windows® Server 2003 and require the version of LDP that ships with Microsoft® Windows® Server 2003.

Installing LDP
From your Microsoft® Windows® Operating System CD, install the Support Tools from the Support\Tools folder by double-clicking the Setup icon.

Starting LDP
There are three ways to start LDP
- Open Windows® 2000 Support Tools menu and select **Active Directory® Administration Tool**
- Execute LDP.exe using **Start | Run**
- Execute LDP.exe from the command prompt

The Scope pane (left) can display the Directory Information Tree (DIT) for navigation.

The Results pane (right) displays the results or error messages of your LDAP operations.

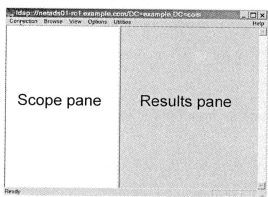

Figure 4.1 – LDP opening screen

Connecting to a Server

To start searching or manipulating the Active Directory® through the LDP tool, you need to connect to the LDAP port on a domain controller. LDP can connect to only one LDAP server at a time.

To connect to the server, open the connect dialog using **Connection | Connect**.

You are prompted for a server name, port number and whether or not you want to connect via a connectionless (UDP) or connection (TCP) oriented protocol. The Active Directory® supports serverless binding which means you can connect and bind to the default server without specifying the name of the server. If you choose the defaults you will connect to the current domain controller that you are authenticated against.

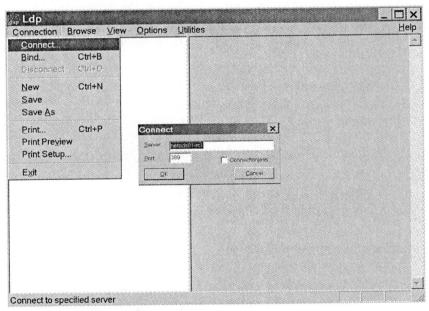

Figure 4.2 – Connection menu

If you wish to connect to another domain controller, specify the server name.

The most common LDAP ports are
      389 is the standard LDAP port and is the default setting
      3268 is the global catalog port
      636 is for SSL

RootDSE

After connecting, LDP queries for and displays RootDSE.

RootDSE (DSA-Specific Entry) is defined for LDAP v3.0 and mandates seven specific attributes to be returned. In addition to the mandatory requirements, a Microsoft® Windows® 2000 or Windows® Server 2003™ domain controller returns additional system information. For clarity we have laid out an explanation and breakdown of the attributes returned by RootDSE. The explanation is then repeated along with the results returned by a RootDSE query.

RootDSE Seven Mandatory Attributes

Mandatory Attributes	
namingContexts	The DN for each of the supported naming contexts
subschemaSubentry	The DN of the subschema entry, for details of the subschema see RFC 2251
altServer	URLs of other servers that may be contacted when this server becomes unavailable. Not specified for Active Directory
supportedExtensions	OIDs identifying supported extensions. If the server does not support any extensions, this attribute will be absent
supportedControls	OIDs for extension controls supported by this directory server
supportedSASLMechanisms	Security mechanisms supported for SASL negotiation (see LDAP RFCs). By default, GSSAPI is supported
supportedLDAPVersions	Supported LDAP versions, Active Directory® supports 2 and 3

RootDSE Additional Attributes

Additional Attributes	
currentTime	The current time on the server
dsServiceName	The DN of the NTDS Settings object
defaultNamingContext	DN for the domain of which this directory server is a member
schemaNamingContext	DN for the schema NC
configurationNamingContext	DN for the configuration NC
rootDomainNamingContext	DN for the root domain, this also names the forest
supportedLDAPPolicies	Supported LDAP management policies. The policy values can be viewed and changed using the command line tool ntdsutil.exe
highestCommittedUSN	Highest Update Sequence Number (USN) committed to the database on this server
dnsHostName	The Fully Qualified Domain Name (FQDN) of the server
ldapServiceName	Service Principal Name (SPN) for the LDAP server. Used for mutual authentication
serverName	DN for the server, as defined in the configuration container
supportedCapabilities	OIDs identifying the supported capabilities of the server
isSynchronized	If TRUE indicates that a domain controller has completed its initial synchronization with its replication partners

Additional Attributes	
isGlobalCatalogReady	If TRUE indicates that a domain controller is advertising itself as a GC. There is a latency between a domain controller being designated as a GC (properties of the NTDS Settings object) and being ready to accept GC queries. The latency depends on the number of domains and replication topology
domainFunctionality [1]	0=Windows 2000 mode, 1=Windows .NET interim mode, 2=Windows .NET mode
forestFunctionality [1]	0=Windows 2000 mode, 1=Windows .NET interim mode, 2=Windows .NET mode
domainControllerFunctionality [1]	0=Windows 2000 mode, 1=Windows .NET interim mode, 2=Windows .NET mode

[1] These attributes are only available on Microsoft® Windows® Server 2003. If the attributes are missing, the value is assumed to be 0 which identifies Microsoft® Windows® 2000 functionality.

TIP: When entering data into an LDP dialog it is often necessary to use a value that is displayed via RootDSE. Cut and paste from the RootDSE results pane into the dialog.

RootDSE is not returned to the results pane in the order illustrated above. In the following table, we have broken down RootDSE returned by our test forest and combined it to include an explanation of each entry.

RootDSE Results and Explanation

RootDSE Attribute and Explanation	RootDSE Returned Results
currentTime: The current time on the server	1> currentTime: 9/15/2002 2:29:32 Pacific Standard Time Pacific Daylight Time;
subschemaSubentry: [2] The DN of the subschema entry, for details of the subschema see RFC 2251	1> subschemaSubentry: CN=Aggregate,CN=Schema, CN=Configuration,DC=example, DC=com;
dsServiceName: The DN of the NTDS Settings object	1> dsServiceName: CN=NTDS Settings, CN=NETADS01-RC1,CN=Servers, CN=London,CN=Sites, CN=Configuration, DC=example,DC=com;
namingContexts: [2] The DN for each of the supported naming contexts	5> namingContexts: DC=example,DC=com; CN=Configuration, DC=example,DC=com; CN=Schema,CN=Configuration, DC=example,DC=com; DC=DomainDnsZones, DC=example,DC=com; DC=ForestDnsZones, DC=example,DC=com;
defaultNamingContext: DN for the domain of which this directory server is a member	1> defaultNamingContext: DC=example,DC=com;
schemaNamingContext: DN for the schema NC	1> schemaNamingContext: CN=Schema,CN=Configuration, DC=example,DC=com;

RootDSE Attribute and Explanation	RootDSE Returned Results
configurationNamingContext: DN for the configuration NC	1> configurationNamingContext: CN=Configuration, DC=example,DC=com;
rootDomainNamingContext: DN for the root domain, this also names the forest	1> rootDomainNamingContext: DC=example,DC=com;
supportedControls: [2] OIDs for extension controls supported by this directory server	20> supportedControl: 1.2.840.113556.1.4.319; 1.2.840.113556.1.4.801; 1.2.840.113556.1.4.473; 1.2.840.113556.1.4.528; 1.2.840.113556.1.4.417; 1.2.840.113556.1.4.619; 1.2.840.113556.1.4.841; 1.2.840.113556.1.4.529; 1.2.840.113556.1.4.805; 1.2.840.113556.1.4.521; 1.2.840.113556.1.4.970; 1.2.840.113556.1.4.1338; 1.2.840.113556.1.4.474; 1.2.840.113556.1.4.1339; 1.2.840.113556.1.4.1340; 1.2.840.113556.1.4.1413; 2.16.840.1.113730.3.4.9; 2.16.840.1.113730.3.4.10; 1.2.840.113556.1.4.1504; 1.2.840.113556.1.4.802;
supportedLDAPVersion: [2] Supported LDAP versions, Active Directory® supports 3 and 2	2> supportedLDAPVersion: 3; 2;

RootDSE Attribute and Explanation	RootDSE Returned Results
supportedLDAPPolicies: Supported LDAP management policies. The policy values can be viewed and changed using the command line tool ntdsutil.exe	11> supportedLDAPPolicies: MaxPoolThreads; MaxDatagramRecv; MaxReceiveBuffer; InitRecvTimeout; MaxConnections; MaxConnIdleTime; MaxPageSize; MaxQueryDuration; MaxTempTableSize; MaxResultSetSize; MaxNotificationPerConn;
highestCommittedUSN: Highest USN committed to the database on this server	1> highestCommittedUSN: 17202;
supportedSASLMechanisms: [2] Security mechanisms supported for SASL negotiation (see LDAP RFCs). By default, GSSAPI is supported	4> supportedSASLMechanisms: GSSAPI; GSS-SPNEGO; EXTERNAL; DIGEST-MD5;
dnsHostName: The FQDN of the server	1> dnsHostName: netads01-rc1.example.com;
ldapServiceName: SPN for the LDAP server. Used for mutual authentication	1> ldapServiceName: example.com: netads01-rc1$@EXAMPLE.COM;
serverName: DN for the server, as defined in the configuration container	1> serverName: CN=NETADS01-RC1,CN=Servers, CN=London,CN=Sites, CN=Configuration,DC=example, DC=com;
supportedCapabilities: OIDs identifying the supported capabilities of the server	3> supportedCapabilities: 1.2.840.113556.1.4.800; 1.2.840.113556.1.4.1670; 1.2.840.113556.1.4.1791;

RootDSE Attribute and Explanation	RootDSE Returned Results
isSynchronized: If TRUE indicates that a domain controller has completed its initial synchronization with its replication partners	1> isSynchronized: TRUE;
isGlobalCatalogReady: If TRUE indicates that a domain controller is advertising itself as a GC. There is latency between a domain controller being designated as a GC (properties of the NTDS Settings object) and being ready to accept GC queries. The latency depends on the number of domains and replication topology	1> isGlobalCatalogReady: TRUE;
domainFunctionality: [1] 0=Windows 2000 mode, 1=Windows .NET Interim mode, 2=Windows .NET mode	1> domainFunctionality: 0;
forestFunctionality: [1] 0=Windows 2000 mode, 1=Windows .NET Interim mode, 2=Windows .NET mode	1> forestFunctionality: 0;
domainControllerFunctionality: [1] 0=Windows 2000 mode, 1=Windows .NET Interim mode, 2=Windows .NET mode	1>domainControllerFunctionality: 2

[1] These attributes are only available on Microsoft® Windows® Server 2003. If the attributes are missing, the value is assumed to be 0 which identifies Microsoft® Windows® 2000 functionality.

[2] Mandatory RFC definitions. Five are listed above and the remaining two are:

Mandatory RFC Attributes	Explanation
altServer:	URLs of other servers that may be contacted when this server becomes unavailable. Not specified for Active Directory®
supportedExtension:	OIDs identifying supported extensions. If the server does not support any extensions, this attribute will be absent

TIP: When writing scripts that require naming context information, it is far more efficient to pull this from RootDSE rather than to hard code it into the script. It comes at the cost of a few more lines of code. This book is not intended to be a scripting one, but a simple script to query RootDSE is:

```
Set objAD = GetObject("LDAP://RootDSE")
n=0
for each NC in objAD.Get("namingContexts")
        n = n + 1
next
buffer =  "There are " & n & " Naming Contexts:"
for each NC in objAD.Get("namingContexts")
        buffer =  buffer & vbCRLf & NC
next
a = MsgBox(buffer, vbOKOnly,"RootDSE Query")
```

TIP: If you don't want to see RootDSE every time you connect LDP to the server, you can disable this in the General Option dialog (**Options | General**). Clear the check box for **Auto default NC query.**

TIP: You don't have to disconnect and reconnect LDP every time you want to display the RootDSE. RootDSE is retrieved when a base search is performed on the Active Directory® using a NULL DN. See Chapter 5, Getting to Grips with Searching.

Binding (authenticating) to a Server

After connecting to the LDAP server and before making any LDAP queries, you must bind. **Connection | Bind**.

The Bind dialog allows the user to submit credentials for authentication to the server. If you do not bind your LDP activities will not work. In the Microsoft® Windows® Server 2003 version of LDP you get a useful comment to advise you to bind: "In order to perform this operation a successful bind must be completed". On the Microsoft® Windows® 2000 version, the operation will fail and there will be no meaningful error message. It's always worth checking that you did bind!

The information that any user will see through LDP is based upon their level of security. Therefore it is important to bind to LDP with the relevant user credentials. If you specify NULL credentials, LDP will assume those of the currently logged on user.

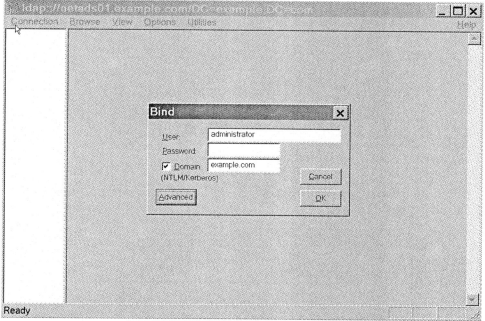

Figure 4.3 – LDP Bind

TIP: To connect and authenticate to the previous server, use the **Bind** option on a disconnected session.

LDP Authentication Methods

There are several methods available in LDP that allows a client to bind to an LDAP server. Open the Bind Options dialog using **Connection | Bind | Advanced**. Remember LDP is a generic tool that allows you to connect to any LDAP server. Consequently, you are given authentication options. For queries against the Active Directory®, we recommend you use the default settings.

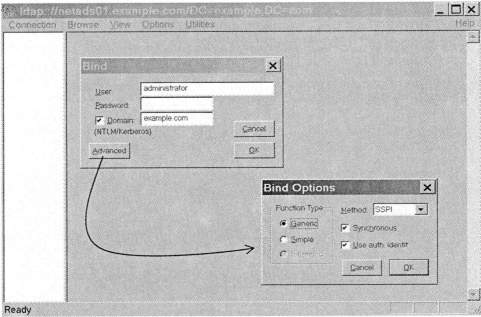

Figure 4.4 – LDP default bind options

If the credentials are left blank LDP will bind using the credentials of the currently logged on user.

When you have performed your bind successfully, you will see a message in the right hand results pane confirming your details:

```
res = ldap_bind_s(ld, NULL, &NtAuthIdentity, 1158); // v.3
        {NtAuthIdentity: User='administrator'; Pwd= <unavailable>;
domain = 'example.com'.}
Authenticated as dn:'administrator'.
```

Disconnecting from the Server

To disconnect from the server select **Connection | Disconnect**. You can now connect to another server or connect as a different user

You can also disconnect by closing the LDP window or choosing **File | Exit**. If you want to retain the information, use the **Save, Save As** or **Print** commands on the File menu before clearing the screen.

When you disconnect from the server, you will see confirmation that you are no longer bound.

```
0x0 = ldap_unbind(ld);
```

TIP: To reduce the noise in the right hand results pane, you can clear it with **Connection | New**. This is not a new server connection; this is a new, clear results window. Remember, if you want to retain the information, use the **Save, Save As** or **Print** commands before clearing it.

TIP: It is possible to disconnect from the existing server and connect and bind to another server without exiting LDP and without losing information in the right hand results pane. This is done by using **Connection | Disconnect**, and then **Connection | Connect, Connection | Bind**.

Menus, Menus, Menus

OK, so we started with some simple options that have opened some of the LDP action/configuration dialogs.

As always there are many ways of getting from A to B. Some shared dialogs within LDP are invoked via different menus. The settings within these dialogs can affect the behaviour of different menu options. As an example LDAP controls can affect both the search and tree view results. Always check the dialogs are set as expected, they can have a significant impact on different menus.

If you follow our examples and invoke the dialogs as required you should not run into any difficulties.

Listed below are the common dialogs and the different menu options for invoking them:

Bind Options
Options | Bind | Options | Bind Options
Connection | Bind | Options | Bind Options

Search Options
Options | Search | Search Options
Browse | Search | Options | Search Options
Browse | Virtual List View | Options | Search Options

Controls
Options | Search | Search Options | Controls
Browse | Search | Options | Controls
Browse | Virtual List View | Options | Controls
Browse | Extended Operations | Controls

Sort Keys
Options | Search | Search Options | Sort Keys
Browse | Search | Options | Sort Keys
Browse | Virtual List View | Options | Sort Keys

Chapter 5 – Getting to Grips with Searching

Searching

To effectively query the Active Directory® you must know:
- Where to start your search (Base Distinguished Name)
- How far and deep to query (Scope)
- What to query for (Search Filters)
- What results to return (Returned Attribute and Values)

There are more advanced settings and we will get to those in time…

Invoke the Search dialog using **Browse | Search**

Where to Start your Search

A directory search always starts at a base distinguished name (Base DN)

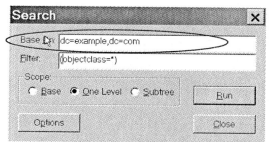

Figure 5.1 – LDP base DN search

The base of a search is set using a Distinguished Name (DN), we have already discussed these. The DN can be set to any object in the Active Directory® and this may be a subcontainer containing child objects or a leaf object.

To query any one of the naming contexts in our example.com forest you would use the corresponding base DN:

Naming Context	Base DN
configuration	cn=configuration,dc=example,dc=com
schema	cn=schema,cn=configuration,dc=example,dc=com
example.com domain	dc=example,dc=com
child.example.com domain	dc=child,dc=example,dc=com

TIP: Copy and paste the appropriate DN from the RootDSE results pane to set the base for your search. It reduces errors and saves your fingers!

How Far and Deep to Query

The scope defines the depth of the search.

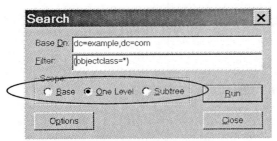

Figure 5.2 – LDP search scope

Base

Searches all the attributes of the selected object

One-level

Searches the attributes of all the direct child objects of the selected container object. Does not search the selected object or through lower level containers.

Subtree

Searches all the attributes of the selected object and all child and grandchild objects.

Selecting the Correct DN and Scope

–   If you know the location of an object that you wish to query, set the DN to the name of the object and perform a base search

–   If you know the name of the container which holds the object, set the base DN to the name of the container and perform a one-level search

–   If you know the top-level container for the subtree which holds the object, set the base DN to the name of the top-level container and perform a subtree search

If you do not know which domain an object resides in, search the global catalog to locate the object. From this search you can retrieve the objects DN.

What to Query for

The search filters specify which attributes should be tested. The specified attributes are tested on all objects within the search scope.

The search filter defines a test condition. If the test evaluates true, the DN of the object is returned together with any requested attributes. LDAP search filters are defined in RFC 2254.

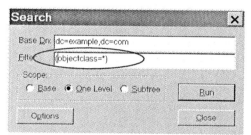

Figure 5.3 – LDP search filter

Search Filter Examples

The results returned will also be dependent on the selected Base DN and Scope.

Filter	Result
cn=johnc	Returns the DNs of the objects where the object's cn attribute is set to johnc

Filter	Result
description=production worker	Returns the DNs of the objects where the object's description attribute is set to production worker

We will return to creating more complex search filters in a moment but for now we will look at how to select which attributes are returned in the results pane.

What Results to Return

The attributes that should be returned are specified in the LDAP query.

In the Search dialog click the **Options** button and you will be overwhelmed with the range of options to choose from. Don't panic, for now we are only interested in controlling the returned attributes.

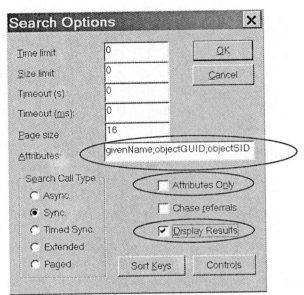

Figure 5.4 – Selecting the attributes to be returned

Before defining which attributes we want returned, there are a couple of other check boxes we would like to explain.

Selecting the **Attributes Only** option specifies that only the names of the populated attributes should be returned. This can be useful when you just want a summary of which attributes are set but not a listing of their values.

It is default for the **Display Results** option to be checked and results are displayed as determined by the **Attributes** field. If the check is removed, only a success or failure notice is displayed with the number of entries found.

The **Attributes** field defines which attributes and associated values are returned in the results pane. When you start LDP for the first time this field is already populated with a number of common attributes, but you will probably want to define your own list.

Each attribute in the **Attributes** field must be separated by a semicolon; do not add any spaces.

For example to display the attribute values of the LDAP display name, common name and description, set the **Attributes** field to:

IDAPDisplayName;cn;description

The values in the **Attributes** field can be defined using either the LDAP display name or the OID that identifies the attribute. The syntax remains the same, OIDs are also separated by semi-colons.

For example, setting the **Attributes** list to:

IDAPDisplayName;cn;description

is equivalent to:

1.2.840.113556.1.2.460;2.5.4.3;2.5.4.13

OK, so you would be popping off the end of the geekometer scale if you specified OIDs unnecessarily, but the 1.1 OID is very useful.

Setting the **Attribute** field to 1.1 specifies that no attributes should be returned. This setting is defined in RFC 2251, section 4.5.1. If you specify no attributes to be returned you just get a list of the DN's of objects for which the search filter evaluates TRUE.

Setting the **Attribute** field to * specifies that all populated attribute values are returned.

Let's do some real searching

All of the following searches are carried out against our test forest as described in Appendix A. So that you can become an LDP guru we suggest that you try these searches out. There are sample scripts in Appendix A that will help you on your way. Remember to do this in a test environment, don't risk a production system!

The initial searches will be based on the England OU.

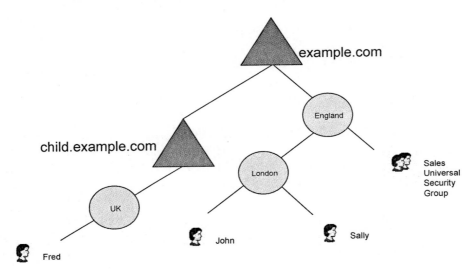

Figure 5.5 – Test forest configuration

Connect to a domain controller in the example domain and bind as the domain administrator.

TIP: To reduce clutter, you can clear the results pane at any time using **Connection | New** or Ctrl + N

Setting the initial search conditions

We want your trial searches to work and we're sure you want the same, so we highly recommend that your copy of LDP is configured in the same way as ours.

Open the Search Options dialog (**Browse | Search | Options**) and configure the settings as follows:

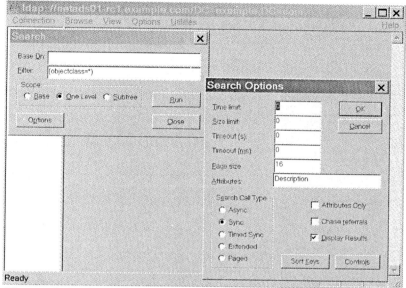

Figure 5.6 – Test forest Search Options dialog

Click on **Sort Keys** and make sure that all the fields in the Sort Keys dialog are blank, if any values appear in the **Active Sort List** field remove them by clicking **<< Check Out**

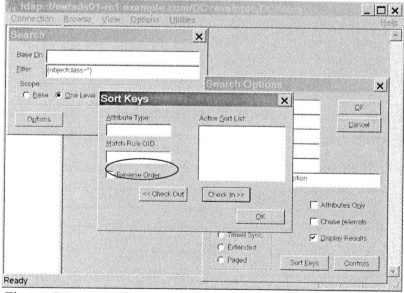

Figure 5.7 – Test forest Sort Keys dialog

Close the Sort Keys dialog and click **Controls** to open the Controls dialog box. Remove any active controls by clicking **<< Check Out**

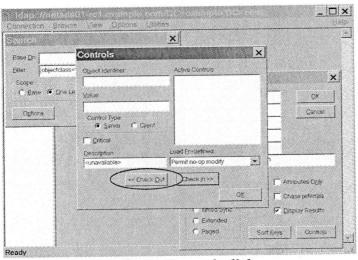

Figure 5.8 – Test forest Controls dialog

Close the Controls and the Search Options dialogs.

Now we are ready to start.

Retrieving RootDSE

The default configuration for LDP is to display RootDSE every time a new connection is made to a server. It does this by making an LDAP query against the server using a NULL base DN.

Set the Search dialog as follows:	
Base DN	
Filter	objectClass=*
Scope	Base
Set the Search Options dialog as follows:	
Attributes	*

Run the search and you will see that RootDSE is returned. Querying RootDSE yourself gives you more flexibility as you can choose which attributes are returned.

Searching for Attribute Values

Set the Search dialog as follows:	
Base DN	ou=england,dc=example,dc=com
Filter	description=*
Scope	Base
Set the Search Options dialog as follows:	
Attributes	*

The filter will evaluate TRUE for all objects that have their description attribute set to a value. If the filter evaluates TRUE, the DN of the object is returned along with any requested attributes that have values set. Attributes with no values are not displayed.

Our results pane displays the following:

```
***Searching...
ldap_search_s(ld, "ou=england,dc=example,dc=com", 0,
"Description=*", attrList,  0, &msg)
Result <0>: (null)
Matched DNs:
Getting 1 entries:
>> Dn: OU=England,DC=example,DC=com
        2> objectClass: top; organizationalUnit;
        1> ou: England;
        1> description: Great Country;
        1> distinguishedName: OU=England,DC=example,DC=com;
        1> instanceType: 4;
        1> whenCreated: 9/12/2002 8:2:37 Pacific Standard Time Pacific
Daylight Time;
        1> whenChanged: 9/12/2002 8:2:37 Pacific Standard Time
Pacific Daylight Time;
        1> uSNCreated: 16020;
        1> uSNChanged: 16021;
        1> name: England;
        1> objectGUID: b23293bb-fab9-407d-8de2-72905f158a00;
objectCategory: CN=Organizational-
Unit,CN=Schema,CN=Configuration,DC=example,DC=com;
```

In the previous example we returned all attributes with values. You can select an individual attribute to be returned by setting the Search Options appropriately.

For the next example, configure the attributes field so only the description is returned.

Set the Search Options dialog as follows:	
Attributes	description

Testing out the Scope

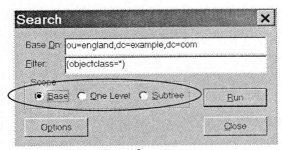

Figure 5.9 – Search scopes

With the **Base** scope selected, run the search. The search is performed against the object identified by the base DN.

The results pane shows:

```
Getting 1 entries:
>> Dn: OU=England,DC=example,DC=com
        1> description: Great Country;
```

Select the **One Level** scope and run the search. The search is performed against direct descendants of the object identified by the base DN (the base object is not included).

The results pane shows:

```
Getting 1 entries:
>> Dn: OU=London,OU=England,DC=example,DC=com
description: Great City;
```

Select the **Subtree** scope and run the search. The search is performed against all objects in the subtree including the base object.

The results pane shows:

```
Getting 3 entries:
>> Dn: OU=England,DC=example,DC=com
        1> description: Great Country;
>> Dn: OU=London,OU=England,DC=example,DC=com
        1> description: Great City;
>> Dn: CN=Sally,OU=London,OU=England,DC=example,DC=com
description: Great Lady;
```

The DN of the user account object called John is not returned, there is no description set for John and consequently the filter did not evaluate TRUE.

Defining the Attributes to be Returned

Set the Search Options dialog as follows:	
Attributes	1.1

The 1.1 OID specifies that only the DNs (no attributes) are returned.

Run the search again and you will see that only the DNs of the objects for which the filter evaluates TRUE are returned.

The results pane will show:

Getting 3 entries:
>> Dn: OU=England,DC=example,DC=com
>> Dn: OU=London,OU=England,DC=example,DC=com
>> Dn: CN=Sally,OU=London,OU=England,DC=example,DC=com

To see all attributes that have values set:

Set the Search Options dialog as follows:
Attributes	★

To list of all of the attributes that have values but not display the actual values, open the **Search Options** dialog and select the **Attributes Only** option.

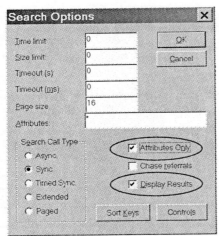

Figure 5.10 – Search options, attributes only and display results

If you want to perform the query but don't want to display the results, clear the **Display Results** option.

To specify a number of different attributes to be returned, enter them into the **Attribute** field separated by semicolons. Do not add any spaces between attributes.

Set the Search Options dialog as follows:	
Attributes	givenName;objectGUID;objectSID

To return results on all objects, you will need a filter that evaluates TRUE regardless of object type:

Set the Search dialog as follows:	
Base DN	ou=england,dc=example,dc=com
Filter	objectClass=*
Scope	Subtree

Run the search and you will see:

```
Getting 4 entries:
>> Dn: OU=England,DC=example,DC=com
        1> objectGUID: 77018f02-d9db-4d42-a3a4-a2c25ca88ec4;
>> Dn: OU=London,OU=England,DC=example,DC=com
        1> objectGUID: 6ad20a38-e4b2-4183-9ea3-a0c4eb254a1f;
>> Dn: CN=Sally,OU=London,OU=England,DC=example,DC=com
        1> objectGUID: 35d263d4-de5a-456a-8460-9092d24d5b64;
        1> objectSid: S-1-5-21-2028412816-169293551-324148440-1139;
>> Dn: CN=John,OU=London,OU=England,DC=example,DC=com
        1>  objectGUID: 9d7de7a1-c835-44e1-8984-464ac75e5509;
        1>  objectSid: S-1-5-21-2028412816-169293551-324148440-1140;
```

Locating Directory Objects by GUIDs and SIDs

In addition to the DN each directory object is identified by a GUID, security principals also have a SID. Looking back at the last results you will notice that Sally and John both have SIDs but the two OUs don't. (The values of the GUID and SIDs will be different on your system.)

In this section we will look at using GUIDs and SIDs to define the search base.

If an object is moved or renamed then its DN changes but its GUID remains the same. The SID will remain the same unless the object is moved to another domain in the forest; the movetree.exe utility can be used to move objects between domains.

Examples of Setting the Search Base Using a GUID or SID

Before you try out the next searches you need the GUID and SID for John. Run the last search again and from the results pane copy and paste the GUID and SID into a Notepad window. Now change John's DN by moving him to the root of the domain. If you are using Server 2003, drag-and-drop John to the root of the domain; if you are using Microsoft® Windows® 2000 right-click John's account object and select move.

In the Search dialog set the base DN to John's GUID, use the following format:

Set the Search dialog as follows:	
Base DN	<GUID=9d7de7a1-c835-44e1-8984-464ac75e5509>
Filter	objectClass=*
Scope	Base

Run the search and you will see that John is immediately located and the new DN is displayed:

```
Getting 1 entries:
>> Dn: CN=John,DC=example,DC=com
        1> objectGUID: 9d7de7a1-c835-44e1-8984-464ac75e5509;
        1> objectSid: S-1-5-21-2028412816-169293551-324148440-1140;
```

If you had used the GUID for the England OU, this would have set the base for the search and you would have been able to display sub-objects by selecting the appropriate scope.

Repeat the search, using John's SID:

Set the Search dialog as follows:	
Base DN	<SID= S-1-5-21-2028412816-169293551-324148440-1140>
Filter	objectClass=*
Scope	Base

Run the search and you will see that John is again immediately located and the DN is displayed:

Searching for objects via a SID is very effective. We have often used this technique to locate the user associated with an "account unknown" SID that appears in the file system or Active Directory® security ACL editor. Are you familiar with this?

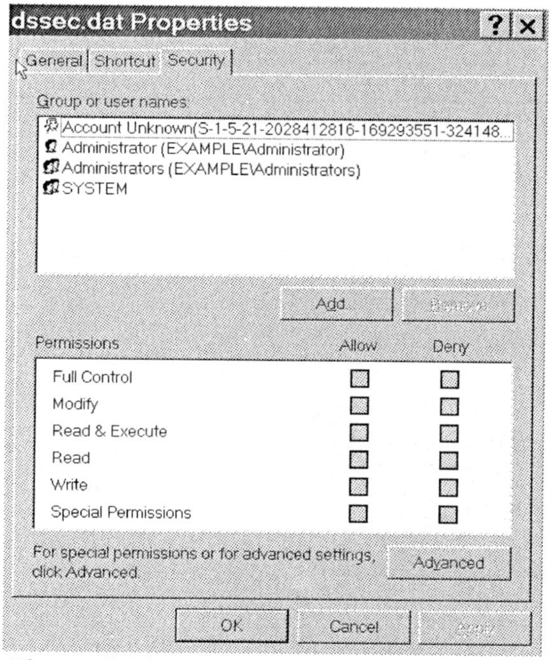

Figure 5.11 – Account unknown

In these circumstances a straight forward search for the object using its SID will probably fail. Most often the SID is displayed because the associated security principal object has been deleted. To see deleted objects you need to use an LDAP control, see Deleted Objects in Chapter 7, Controlling Returned Results.

SIDs and RIDs

The stem of the SID identifies the domain and the last part of the SID (1140 in our example) is referred to as the RID. The RIDs are allocated from a pool controlled by the RID master.

The *rIDAvailablePool* attribute of the RID Manager$ object identifies the start value of the next RID pool that will be allocated to a DC and also the maximum number of RIDs that can be allocated per domain.

To retrieve this value:

Set the Search dialog as follows:	
Base DN	cn=rid manager$,cn=system,dc=example,dc=com
Filter	objectClass=*
Scope	Base
Set the Search Options dialog as follows:	
Attributes	rIDAvailablePool

> Getting 1 entries:
> >> Dn: cn=rid manager$,cn=system,dc=example,dc=com
> rIDAvailablePool: 4611686014132422710;

This returns the value **4611686014132422710** which is stored in a 64-bit large integer. The numeric value of the lower 32-bits specifies the start of the next RID pool to be allocated and the value of the upper 32-bits specifies the maximum number of RIDs that can be allocated in the domain.

To calculate the values convert the number to HEX:

$$4611686014132422710 = 3FFFFFFF00000836.$$

Lower value: **836** (hex) = **2102** (decimal). The start of the next RID pool

Upper value: **3FFFFFFF** (hex) = **1073741823** (decimal). The maximum number of RIDs that can be allocated)

OK so we are geeks, there is an easier way – use LDP's Large Integer Converter. **Utilities | Large Integer Converter.**

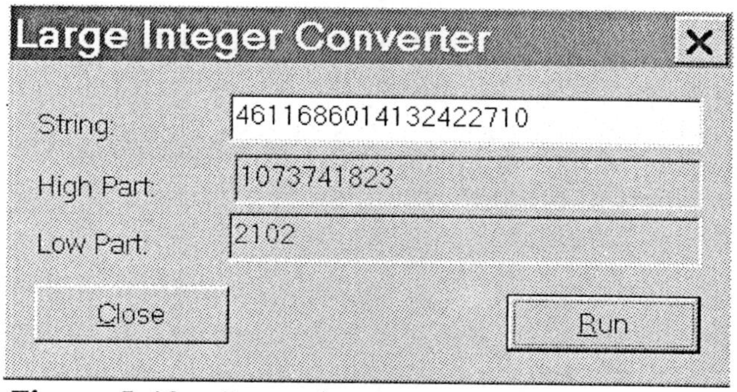

Figure 5.12 – Large integer converter

Locating Server GUIDs within a Domain

The server GUID works in the same way as any other GUID. It is a unique identifier for a server object. It is used primarily to locate a domain controller for the purposes of replication. To search for it, we need to query the configuration naming context where the domain controller settings are held.

Set the Search dialog as follows:	
Base DN	cn=configuration,dc=example,dc=com
Filter	cn=NTDS settings
Scope	Subtree
Attributes	objectGUID

Run the search and you will see the following results:

```
Getting 3 entries:
>> Dn: CN=NTDS Settings,CN=NETADS01-
RC1,CN=Servers,CN=London,
CN=Sites,CN=Configuration,DC=example,DC=com
        1> objectGUID: ecaf8b37-bfcc-4b91-804c-de45e6cb1b80;
>> Dn: CN=NTDS Settings,CN=NETADS02-
RC1,CN=Servers,CN=NewYork,
CN=Sites,CN=Configuration,DC=example,DC=com
        1> objectGUID: f615ca69-c421-4a22-83ce-1bbb1990a3e0;
>> Dn: CN=NTDS Settings,CN=NETADS03-
RC1,CN=Servers,CN=NewYork,
CN=Sites,CN=Configuration,DC=example,DC=com
        1> objectGUID: 71baf083-80d5-4447-a716-5baf333db889;
```

LDAP referrals

If a search is made for an object that does not live within the naming context hosted by the domain controller, the domain controller can issue a referral if it is aware of the location of the object.

With LDP still connected to the server in the example.com domain:

Set the Search dialog as follows:	
Base DN	dc=child,dc=example,dc=com
Filter	cn=Fred
Scope	Subtree

Here we are looking for all objects in the child domain which have their common name attribute set to Fred. This LDAP query is sent to the domain controller in the example.com domain.

Run the search and you will see a search referral error:

```
Error: Search: Referral<10>
```

To chase the referral and resolve the query, open the Search Options dialog and select **Chase referrals**.

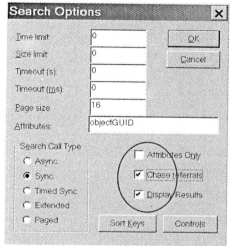

Figure 5.13 – Chase referrals

Run the search and you will see the following results:

```
Getting 1 entries:
>> Dn: CN=Fred,OU=UK,DC=child,DC=example,DC=com
        1> objectGUID: ef544e67-9dbc-45e7-ad09-dc5588b32843;
```

Forest Wide Global Catalog Search

If you want to locate an object but you are not sure which domain naming context contains the object you can search the GC. The GC contains all the objects from the domain NCs in the forest but only a limited set of attributes. When you locate an object, you can retrieve the DN. It may then be necessary to bind to the object in the appropriate domain NC in order to recover the attribute values that you are interested in.

Our user Fred has an account in the child.example.com, but let's pretend we don't know that.

Set the Search dialog as follows:	
Base DN	dc=example,dc=com
Filter	cn=fred
Scope	Subtree

Run the search and you get an error that the object is not found.

To run the search against the GC, use the Connection menu to Disconnect and then reconnect to the GC port 3268. Once you have reconnected don't forget to bind.

Run the search and you will see the following results:

```
Getting 1 entries:
>> Dn: CN=Fred,OU=UK,DC=child,DC=example,DC=com
        1> objectGUID: ef544e67-9dbc-45e7-ad09-dc5588b32843;
```

You now have the DN for Fred and can bind appropriately to recover all the attributes that you require.

Chapter 6 – Advanced Searching with Complex Filters

Complex Search Filters

So far we have shown you a number of simple search filters that contain a single expression. The filter tested a single attribute on an object to see if it was set to a particular value. If the test evaluated TRUE the object's DN was retrieved along with any requested attributes.

In this chapter we will show you how to create more complex search filters so that you can retrieve exactly the information you want. Before constructing and using complex search filters against large directories, review Chapter 10, Tips on Creating Efficient Searches.

Logical Operators

There are a number of LDAP search filter operators that allow different equality tests to be made:

Logical Operators	Description
=	Equal
~=	Approximately equal
<=	Less than or equal to
>=	Greater than or equal to
&	AND
|	OR
!	NOT

Wildcards can be used when specifying values:

Value	Description
jo	Exactly jo
jo*	Starting with jo
*jo	Ending with jo
jo	Containing jo

Filters can be constructed using multiple expressions (tests) and the results of the individual expressions can be combined using logical operators. If the overall filter evaluates TRUE the results are displayed.

Logical operators are placed in front of the expressions to be tested:

The NOT Operator
> Filter 1: (expression A)
> Filter 1: evaluates TRUE if expression A is TRUE
>
> Filter 2: (!(expressionA))
> Filter 2: evaluates TRUE if expression A is FALSE

To list all the objects in the England OU that did not have the *description* attribute set:

Set the Search dialog as follows:	
Base DN	ou=england,dc=example,dc=com
Filter	(!(description=*))
Scope	Subtree
Attributes	1.1

The OR Operator
> Filter 3: (|(expression A)(expression B))
> Filter 3: evaluates true if (expression A) OR (expression B) are TRUE

The operator applies to all of the expressions contained within the outside parentheses

> Filter 4: (|(expression A)(expression B)(expression C)(expression D))
> Filter 4: evaluates true if ANY of the contained expressions are TRUE

To list all of the computers, users and OUs in our directory:

Set the Search dialog as follows:	
Base DN	dc=example,dc=com
Filter	(|(objectCategory=computer)(objectCategory=user)(objectCategory=organizationalUnit))
Scope	Subtree
Attributes	1.1

This can return more objects than expected because the filter is using the *objectCategory* attribute, for more details see *objectClass* and *objectCategory* in Chapter 3 and also later in this chapter.

The AND Operator
> Filter 5: (&(expression A)(expression B)(expression C)(expression D))
> Filter 5 evaluates true if ALL of the contained expressions are TRUE

As you would expect you can combine logical operators:

To list all of the computers and users in our directory that have a description set:

Set the Search dialog as follows:	
Base DN	dc=example,dc=com
Filter	(&(description=*)(|(objectCategory=computer)(objectCategory=user)))
Scope	Subtree
Attributes	Description

To list all of the computers and users in our directory that do not have a description set:

Set the Search dialog as follows:	
Base DN	dc=example,dc=com
Filter	(&(!(description=*))(|(objectCategory=computer)(objectCategory=user)))
Scope	Subtree
Attributes	Description

objectClass and objectCategory

In the above examples we have set the value of the *objectCategory* attribute to the LDAP display name of the object class. If you looked at the value contained in an *objectCategory* attribute you would find that it was a DN (eg. cn=person,cn=schema,cn=configuration,dc=example,dc=com). So how do we get away with setting the value to an LDAP display name? The answer is that the server looks up the object referenced by the LDAP display name in the schema, retrieves the *objectCategory* attribute value and changes the filter to use the DN.

The *objectCategory* attribute value is the same for a number of different object classes. The *objectCategory* attribute value for *user, contact, organizationalPerson, person* and *inetOrgPerson* are all set to:

cn=person,cn=schema,cn=configuration,<dc=forestroot>

Consequently searching using a filter set to (objectCategory=user) returns all of the above "people".

But what if you just wanted to find user objects? Using (objectClass=user) doesn't solve the problem, *objectClass* is a multi-valued attribute containing the name of the class definition and all of the parent classes. A search on (objectClass=user) will return both user and computer objects. Computer objects are returned because user is the parent class for a computer object. See *objectClass* and *ObjectCategory* in Chapter 3.

To create a search that just returns user objects you must set up the following filter:

Set the Search dialog as follows:	
Base DN	dc=example,dc=com
Filter	(&(objectClass=user)(objectCategory=user))
Scope	Subtree
Attributes	Description

Reserved Characters

There will be times when you want to search for values that contain reserved characters. This requires representing the character in hex and prefixing it with a backslash (\).

Required character	Escape sequence
*	\2a
(	\28
)	\29
\	\5c
NUL	\00

If you wanted to search for all user descriptions ending in a closing parenthesis ")" the following filter will fail

(&(objectCategory=user)(description=*))).

The parenthesis after the * must be replaced with the appropriate escape sequence

(&(objectCategory=user)(description=*\29))

Enumerating all the Schema Object Definitions

Use the following search to list all of the objects that are defined in the schema.

Set the Search dialog as follows:	
Base DN	cn=schema,cn=configuration,dc=example,dc=com
Filter	(objectCategory=classSchema)
Scope	Subtree
Attributes	lDAPDisplayName

On Microsoft® Windows® Server 2003 (RC1) you would find that there are 189

Enumerating all the Schema Attribute Definitions

Use the following search to list all of the attributes that are defined in the schema.

Set the Search dialog as follows:	
Base DN	cn=schema,cn=configuration,dc=example,dc=com
Filter	(objectCategory=attributeSchema)
Scope	Subtree
Attributes	lDAPDisplayName

If you observe the results pane, you will see (watch carefully as it scrolls past pretty quickly):

```
Error: Search: Size Limit Exceeded. <4>
Result <4>: (null)
Matched DNs:   Getting 1000 entries:
```

If you scroll back in the result pane to view the message you will see that it has been lost. There are two issues:

- The first issue is that the server will only return 1000 entries (this is set by the server side LDAP policy MaxPageSize)
- The second issue is that LDP is initially configured to only buffer 512 lines

These issues are dealt with in Chapter 7, Controlling Returned Results. For now we will increase the buffer size and page the returned results.

Open the General Options dialog in LDP using **Options | General** and set the number of lines to 4000. LDP will now let you scroll through 4000 lines of results.

To page the returned results, from the LDP Search dialog click **Options** and configure the dialog as illustrated.

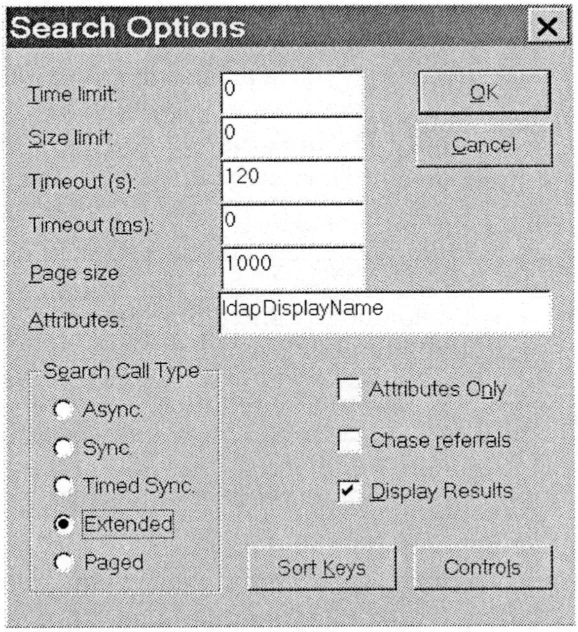

Figure 6.1 – Page size configuration

Run the query again and 1000 results will be returned and you will be prompted as follows:

```
-=>> 'Run' for more, 'Close' to abandon <<=-
```

Click **Run** and you will see another set of results being returned. So you don't confuse further searches set the Search Call Type back to Sync.

Enumerating Category 1 and 2 Objects

If an object definition is part of the base schema then it is a category 1 object. To find all schema extensions requires a search for category 2 objects. The object category is defined by a flag set in the object definition's *systemFlags* attribute. This discussion also applies to attributes because attributes are defined as *attributeSchema* class objects. See Chapter 3 for more details.

Matching rules (see Chapter 3) are required to test the *systemFlags*. If bit 4 is set the object is category 1, if it is clear the object is category 2.

To enumerate category 1 objects:

Set the Search dialog as follows:	
Base DN	cn=schema,cn=configuration,dc=example,dc=com
Filter	(systemFlags:1.2.840.113556.1.4.803:=16)
Scope	Subtree
Attributes	lDAPDisplayName

To enumerate category 2 objects (schema extensions):

Set the Search dialog as follows:	
Base DN	cn=schema,cn=configuration,dc=example,dc=com
Filter	(!(systemFlags:1.2.840.113556.1.4.803:=16))
Scope	Subtree
Attributes	lDAPDisplayName

Enumerating Attributes Replicated to the GC

All objects in the forest are replicated to the GC but the GC only holds a limited number of attributes.

If an attribute is replicated to the GC then the *isMemberOfPartialAttributeSet* property of the *attributeSchema* definition is set TRUE.

To enumerate all the attributes that are replicated to the GC, run the search below.

Set the Search dialog as follows:	
Base DN	cn=schema,cn=configuration,dc=example,dc=com
Filter	(&(objectCategory=attributeSchema)(isMemberOfPartialAttributeSet=TRUE))
Scope	Subtree
Attributes	IDAPDisplayName

The results set will look something like this (we are only showing a sample of the overall set):

```
Getting 151 entries:
>> Dn: CN=Alt-Security-
Identities,CN=Schema,CN=Configuration,DC=example,DC=com
        1> IDAPDisplayName: altSecurityIdentities;
>> Dn: CN=CA-
Certificate,CN=Schema,CN=Configuration,DC=example,DC=com
        1> IDAPDisplayName: cACertificate;
>> Dn: CN=CA-Certificate-
DN,CN=Schema,CN=Configuration,DC=example,DC=com
        1> IDAPDisplayName: cACertificateDN;
>> Dn: CN=Certificate-
Templates,CN=Schema,CN=Configuration,DC=example,DC=com
        1> IDAPDisplayName: certificateTemplates;
```

140 attributes are replicated to the GC in a newly installed Microsoft® Windows® 2000 system and 151 attributes in Microsoft® Windows® Server 2003.

Enumerating Indexed Attributes

It is much more efficient to query indexed attributes when searching the Active Directory®. An attribute is indexed by setting the appropriate flag (bit) in the *searchFlags* property of the *attributeSchema* definition.

Matching rules are required to test the *searchFlags*. If bit 0 is set then an attribute is indexed. See Chapter 3, Matching Rules and Search Flags for more details.

Set the Search dialog as follows:	
Base DN	cn=schema,cn=configuration,dc=example,dc=com
Filter	(&(objectCategory=attributeSchema)(searchFlags:1.2.840.113556.1.4.803:=1))
Scope	Subtree
Attributes	lDAPDisplayName

64 attributes are indexed in a newly installed Microsoft® Windows® 2000 system and 69 attributes are indexed in Microsoft® Windows® Server 2003.

Enumerating Members of the ANR Set.

An attribute can be included in ANR searches. An attribute is added to ANR searches by setting the appropriate flags (bits) in the *searchFlags* property of the *attributeSchema* definition.

Matching rules are required to test the *searchFlags*. If bit 0 and bit 2 are set the attribute is a member of the ANR set.

To see all members of the ANR set:

Set the Search dialog as follows:	
Base DN	cn=schema,cn=configuration,dc=example,dc=com
Filter	(&(objectCategory=attributeSchema)(searchFlags:1.2.840.113556.1.4.803:=5))
Scope	Subtree
Attributes	lDAPDisplayName

8 attributes are included in the ANR set in a newly installed Microsoft® Windows® 2000 system and 9 are included in Microsoft® Windows® Server 2003.

Identifying Control Access Rights

Control access rights include property sets, extended rights and validated writes. These are all defined using *controlAccessRight* objects that are created in the cn=extended-rights,cn=configuration,dc=example,dc=com container.

You can tell whether a *controlAccessRight* object represents a property set, extended right or validated write by the value stored in the object's *validAccesses* attribute.

controlAccessRight	*validAccesses* attribute value (decimal)
Property set	48
Extended right	256
Validated write	8

To identify all the property sets

Set the Search dialog as follows:	
Base DN	cn=extended-rights,cn=configuration,dc=example,dc=com
Filter	(validAccesses=48)
Scope	Subtree
Attributes	displayName

You will see that there are 12 system defined property sets. The name in the security user interface to control access to the property set is returned in the *displayName* attribute.

```
Getting 12 entries:
>> Dn: CN=DNS-Host-Name-Attributes,CN=Extended-
Rights,CN=Configuration,DC=example,DC=com
        1> displayName: DNS Host Name Attributes;
>> Dn: CN=Domain-Other-Parameters,CN=Extended-
Rights,CN=Configuration,DC=example,DC=com
        1> displayName: Other Domain Parameters (for use by SAM);
>> Dn: CN=Domain-Password,CN=Extended-
Rights,CN=Configuration,DC=example,DC=com
        1> displayName: Domain Password & Lockout Policies;
>> Dn: CN=Email-Information,CN=Extended-
Rights,CN=Configuration,DC=example,DC=com
        1> displayName: Phone and Mail Options;
>> Dn: CN=General-Information,CN=Extended-
Rights,CN=Configuration,DC=example,DC=com
        1> displayName: General Information;
>> Dn: CN=Membership,CN=Extended-
Rights,CN=Configuration,DC=example,DC=com
        1> displayName: Group Membership;
>> Dn: CN=Personal-Information,CN=Extended-
Rights,CN=Configuration,DC=example,DC=com
        1> displayName: Personal Information;
>> Dn: CN=Public-Information,CN=Extended-
Rights,CN=Configuration,DC=example,DC=com
        1> displayName: Public Information;
>> Dn: CN=RAS-Information,CN=Extended-
Rights,CN=Configuration,DC=example,DC=com
        1> displayName: Remote Access Information;
>> Dn: CN=User-Account-Restrictions,CN=Extended-
Rights,CN=Configuration,DC=example,DC=com
        1> displayName: Account Restrictions;
>> Dn: CN=User-Logon,CN=Extended-
Rights,CN=Configuration,DC=example,DC=com
        1> displayName: Logon Information;
>> Dn: CN=Web-Information,CN=Extended-
Rights,CN=Configuration,DC=example,DC=com
displayName: Web Information;
```

If you change the filter to look for extended rights you will find there are 48 and you will also find that there are three validated writes.

Identifying the Objects to which a Control Access Right applies

The *controlAccessRight* object has an *appliesTo* attribute which is multi-valued and contains the *schemaIDGUID* for each of the objects associated with the *controlAccessRight* object.

In our example we will find all the objects to which the personal information property set applies to.

You first need to retrieve the *appliesTo* attribute value for the Personal Information *controlAccessRight* object. The DN of the object is:

> cn=Personal-Information,cn=Extended-Rights,
> cn=Configuration,dc=example,dc=com

You can retrieve the *appliesTo* value using LDP either by searching or using the tree view mode, see Chapter 9, A Different Way of Seeing and Doing Things.

Another method of retrieving this value would be to use ADSI Edit. This has the advantage of displaying the syntax of the attribute value. If the syntax is shown as unicode string the value is stored in GUID string format. The other format is shown as octet string (see Chapter 3 for more details on formats).

Set the Search dialog as follows:	
Base DN	cn=personal-information,cn=extended-rights,cn=configuration,dc=example,dc=com
Filter	(objectClass=*)
Scope	Base
Attributes	appliesTo

Getting 1 entries:
>>Dn:CN=Personal-Information,CN=Extended-Rights,CN=Configuration,DC=example,DC=com
    4> appliesTo: 4828CC14-1437-45bc-9B07-AD6F015E5F28; bf967a86-0de6-11d0-a285-00aa003049e2; 5cb41ed0-0e4c-11d0-a286-00aa003049e2; bf967aba-0de6-11d0-a285-00aa003049e2;

The results show us that the Personal Information property set applies to four different object types. The object types are identified by the four GUIDs returned.

The *appliesTo* value is stored in GUID string format and the *SchemaIDGUID* is stored in binary octet string. Before you can search for a matching *SchemaIDGUID* value you must convert the string. See Chapter 3, GUIDs for information on string conversion.

GUID string	4828CC14-1437-45bc-9B07-AD6F015E5F28
Binary octet string	14 cc 28 48 37 14 bc 45 9b 07 ad 6f 01 5e 5f 28

To use the binary octet string in a search filter every byte must be preceded by the backslash escape character:

\14\cc\28\48\37\14\bc\45\9b\07\ad\6f\01\5e\5f\28

You can now run your search using LDP

Set the Search dialog as follows:	
Base DN	cn=schema,cn=configuration,dc=example,dc=com
Filter	(&(objectClass=classSchema)(schemaIDGUID=\14\cc\28\48\37\14\bc\45\9b\07\ad\6f\01\5e\5f\28))
Scope	Subtree
Attributes	ldapDisplayName

This returns:

```
Getting 1 entries:
>> Dn:
CN=inetOrgPerson,CN=Schema,CN=Configuration,DC=example,DC=com
        1> lDAPDisplayName: inetOrgPerson;
```

The remaining GUIDs convert to:

```
\86\7a\96\bf\e6\0d\d0\11\a2\85\00\aa\00\30\49\e2
\d0\1e\b4\5c\4c\0e\d0\11\a2\86\00\aa\00\30\49\e2
\ba\7a\96\bf\e6\0d\d0\11\a2\85\00\aa\00\30\49\e2
```

Use them in the search filter and you will find the three other objects with which the personal information property set can be used. The LDAP display names for the four objects are:

- *inetOrgPerson*
- *computer*
- *contact*
- *user*

Identifying all the Control Access Rights associated with an Object Class

The GUID value held in the *schemaIDGUID* attribute of an object class definition is used to identify which control access rights are associated with that object class. If a control access right is associated with a particular class then the class's *SchemaIDGUID* value is stored in the *appliesTo* attribute of the *controlAccessRight* object.

In our example we will enumerate all the control access rights that are associated with a user object.

You first need to retrieve the *schemaIDGUID* value for the user class definition.

You can retrieve the GUID using LDP either by searching or using the Tree view mode.

Set the Search dialog as follows:	
Base DN	cn=user,cn=schema,cn=configuration,dc=example,dc=com
Filter	(ObjectClass=*)
Scope	Base
Attributes	schemaIDGUID

```
Getting 1 entries:
>> Dn:
CN=User,CN=Schema,CN=Configuration,DC=example,DC=com
        1> schemaIDGUID: bf967aba-0de6-11d0-a285-00aa003049e2;
```

To enumerate all property sets associated with this object, you need to search for *controlAccessRight* objects which have their *appliesTo* attribute set to the GUID. The *appliesTo* attribute value is stored in GUID string format and there is no need to translate it

Set the Search dialog as follows:	
Base DN	cn=extended-rights,cn=configuration,dc=example,dc=com
Filter	(appliesTo=bf967aba-0de6-11d0-a285-00aa003049e2)
Scope	Subtree
Attributes	displayName

You will see 14 results returned. These 14 results identify the property sets, extended rights and validated writes that are associated with user objects. To identify the individual *controlAccessRight* object types you need to refine the filter.

You can tell whether a *controlAccessRight* object represents a property set, extended right or validated write by the value stored in the object's *validAccesses* attribute.

controlAccessRight	*validAccesses* attribute value (decimal)
Property set	48
Extended right	256
Validated write	8

To identify all Property Sets associated with a User Object:

Set the Search dialog as follows:	
Base DN	cn=extended-rights,cn=configuration,dc=example,dc=com
Filter	(&(validaccesses=48)(appliesTo=bf967aba-0de6-11d0-a285-00aa003049e2))
Scope	Subtree
Attributes	displayName

```
Matched DNs:
Getting 9 entries:
>> Dn: CN=RAS-Information,CN=Extended-
Rights,CN=Configuration,DC=example,DC=com
        1> displayName: Remote Access Information;
>> Dn: CN=General-Information,CN=Extended-
Rights,CN=Configuration,DC=example,DC=com
        1> displayName: General Information;
>> Dn: CN=User-Account-Restrictions,CN=Extended-
Rights,CN=Configuration,DC=example,DC=com
        1> displayName: Account Restrictions;
>> Dn: CN=User-Logon,CN=Extended-
Rights,CN=Configuration,DC=example,DC=com
        1> displayName: Logon Information;
>> Dn: CN=Membership,CN=Extended-
Rights,CN=Configuration,DC=example,DC=com
        1> displayName: Group Membership;
>> Dn: CN=Personal-Information,CN=Extended-
Rights,CN=Configuration,DC=example,DC=com
        1> displayName: Personal Information;
>> Dn: CN=Email-Information,CN=Extended-
Rights,CN=Configuration,DC=example,DC=com
        1> displayName: Phone and Mail Options;
>> Dn: CN=Web-Information,CN=Extended-
Rights,CN=Configuration,DC=example,DC=com
        1> displayName: Web Information;
>> Dn: CN=Public-Information,CN=Extended-
Rights,CN=Configuration,DC=example,DC=com
displayName: Public Information;
```

To identify all Extended Rights associated with a User Object:

Set the Search dialog as follows:	
Base DN	cn=extended-rights,cn=configuration,dc=example,dc=com
Filter	(&(validaccesses=256)(appliesTo=bf967aba-0de6-11d0-a285-00aa003049e2))
Scope	Subtree
Attributes	displayName

Matched DNs:
Getting 5 entries:
>> Dn: CN=Allowed-To-Authenticate,CN=Extended-Rights,CN=Configuration,DC=example,DC=com
    1> displayName: Allowed to Authenticate;
>> Dn: CN=User-Change-Password,CN=Extended-Rights,CN=Configuration,DC=example,DC=com
    1> displayName: Change Password;
>> Dn: CN=User-Force-Change-Password,CN=Extended-Rights,CN=Configuration,DC=example,DC=com
    1> displayName: Reset Password;
>> Dn: CN=Send-As,CN=Extended-Rights,CN=Configuration,DC=example,DC=com
    1> displayName: Send As;
>> Dn: CN=Receive-As,CN=Extended-Rights,CN=Configuration,DC=example,DC=com
displayName: Receive As;

To identify all Validated Writes associated with a User Object:

Set the Search dialog as follows:	
Base DN	cn=extended-rights,cn=configuration,dc=example,dc=com
Filter	(&(validaccesses=4)(appliesTo=bf967aba-0de6-11d0-a285-00aa003049e2))
Scope	Subtree
Attributes	displayName

Matched DNs:
Getting 0 entries:

There are no validated writes associated with user objects. Only three validated writes are defined for the system and these cannot be extended. One validated write is applied to group objects and two apply to computer objects. See Control Access Rights in Chapter 3.

Enumerating Members of the same Property Set

This search will identify all the members of a particular property set. Property set members are identified by a GUID. The GUID is stored in:

— The *rightsGuid* attribute of the *controlAccessRight* object that defines the property set
— The *SchemaIDGUID* property of each attribute that is a member of the property set

This topic is tricky! See Property Sets in Chapter 3 for further information.

In our example we will find all members of the Personal Information property set.

You first need to retrieve the *rightsGuid* for the Personal Information *controlAccessRight* object. The DN of the object is:

cn=Personal-Information,cn=Extended-Rights,
cn=Configuration,dc=example,dc=com

You can retrieve the *rightsGUID* value using LDP either by searching or using the tree view mode, see Chapter 9, A Different Way of Seeing and Doing Things.

Another method of retrieving this value would be to use ADSI Edit. This has the advantage of displaying the syntax of the attribute value. If the syntax is shown as unicode string, the value is stored in GUID string format. The other format is shown as octet string. See GUIDs in Chapter 3 for more details on formats.

Set the Search dialog as follows:	
Base DN	cn=personal-information,cn=extended-rights,cn=configuration,dc=example,dc=com
Filter	(objectClass=*)
Scope	Base
Attributes	rightsGuid

Getting 1 entries:
>>Dn:
CN=Personal-Information,CN=Extended-Rights,CN=Configuration,DC=example,DC=com
rightsGuid: 77B5B886-944A-11d1-AEBD-0000F80367C1

The *rightsGuid* is stored in GUID string format and the *attributeSecurityGUID* is stored in binary octet string format. Before you can search for matching *attributeSecurityGUID* values you must convert the string.

GUID string	77B5B886-944A-11d1-AEBD-0000F80367C1
Binary octet string	86 B8 B5 77 4A 94 D1 11 AE BD 00 00 F8 03 67 C1

To use an binary octet string in a search filter every byte must be preceded by the backslash escape character:

\86\B8\B5\77\4A\94\D1\11\AE\BD\00\00\F8\03\67\C1

You can now run your search using LDP.

Set the Search dialog as follows:	
Base DN	cn=schema,cn=configuration,dc=example,dc=com
Filter	(&(objectCategory=attributeSchema)(attributeSecurityGUID =\86\B8\B5\77\4A\94\D1\11\AE\BD\00\00\F8\03\67\C1))
Scope	Subtree
Attributes	ldapDisplayName

This will return all the members of the Personal Information property set (we are only showing a sample of the overall set):

Matched DNs:

Getting 41 entries:
>> Dn:
CN=Address,CN=Schema,CN=Configuration,DC=example,DC=com
     1> lDAPDisplayName: streetAddress;
>> Dn: CN=Address-
Home,CN=Schema,CN=Configuration,DC=example,DC=com
     1> lDAPDisplayName: homePostalAddress;
>> Dn:
CN=Assistant,CN=Schema,CN=Configuration,DC=example,DC=com
     1> lDAPDisplayName: assistant;
>> Dn:
CN=Comment,CN=Schema,CN=Configuration,DC=example,DC=com
     1> lDAPDisplayName: info;
>> Dn: CN=Country-
Name,CN=Schema,CN=Configuration,DC=example,DC=com
     1> lDAPDisplayName: c;
>> Dn: CN=Facsimile-Telephone-
Number,CN=Schema,CN=Configuration,DC=example,DC=com
     1> lDAPDisplayName: facsimileTelephoneNumber;
>> Dn: CN=International-ISDN-
Number,CN=Schema,CN=Configuration,DC=example,DC=com
     1> lDAPDisplayName: internationalISDNNumber;
>> Dn: CN=Locality-
Name,CN=Schema,CN=Configuration,DC=example,DC=com
     1> lDAPDisplayName: l;

Identifying Groups

Groups can be located simply based on an *objectCategory* value of *group* or using the *groupType* flags.

The *groupType* is an integer value with individual bits identifying the group characteristics:

Bit	Value	Description of attribute properties
1	2	Set for global groups
2	4	Set for domain local groups
4	8	Set for universal groups
31	2147483648	Set for security groups, clear for distribution groups

To locate all security and distribution groups in our test domain

Set the Search dialog as follows:	
Base DN	dc=example,dc=com
Filter	(objectCategory=group)
Scope	Subtree
Attributes	ldapDisplayName

To locate all security groups in our test domain

Set the Search dialog as follows:	
Base DN	dc=example,dc=com
Filter	(&(objectCategory=group)(groupType:1.2.840.113556.1.4.804:=2147483648))
Scope	Subtree
Attributes	ldapDisplayName

To locate all distribution groups in our test domain

Set the Search dialog as follows:	
Base DN	dc=example,dc=com
Filter	(&(objectCategory=group)(!(groupType:1.2.840.113556.1.4.804:=2147483648)))
Scope	Subtree
Attributes	ldapDisplayName

To locate all universal security groups in our test domain

Set the Search dialog as follows:	
Base DN	dc=example,dc=com
Filter	(&(objectCategory=group)(groupType:1.2.840.113556.1.4.804:=2147483648))
Scope	Subtree
Attributes	ldapDisplayName

To locate all universal distribution groups in our test domain

Set the Search dialog as follows:	
Base DN	dc=example,dc=com
Filter	(&(objectCategory=group)(groupType:1.2.840.113556.1.4.804:=8)(!(groupType:1.2.840.113556.1.4.804:=2147483648)))
Scope	Subtree
Attributes	ldapDisplayName

Identifying Group Policy Objects using a Display Name

This search will return the GUID of a Group Policy Object (GPO). It may be necessary to know the GUID of a GPO when troubleshooting the application of a GP on a domain controller. We are using the Default Domain Policy in this example.

Set the Search dialog as follows:	
Base DN	dc=example,dc=com
Filter	(&(objectCategory=groupPolicyContainer)(displayName=Default Domain Policy))
Scope	Subtree
Attributes	displayName

```
Getting 1 entries:
>> Dn: CN={31B2F340-016D-11D2-945F-
00C04FB984F9},CN=Policies,CN=System,DC=example,DC=com
        1> displayName: Default Domain Policy;
```

Identifying Group Policy Objects using a GUID
This search will return the display name of a GPO where you know the GUID.

Set the Search dialog as follows:	
Base DN	dc=example,dc=com
Filter	(&(objectCategory=groupPolicyContainer)(name={31B2F 340-016D-11D2-945F-00C04FB984F9}))
Scope	Subtree
Attributes	displayName

Identifying all Group Policy Objects
This search will return all GPOs that are contained in the Group Policy Container on the domain controller. In this example there are two default policies, but you would expect many more on an operational domain controller.

Set the Search dialog as follows:	
Base DN	dc=example,dc=com
Filter	objectCategory=groupPolicyContainer
Scope	Subtree
Attributes	displayName

Matched DNs:
Getting 2 entries:
>> Dn: CN={31B2F340-016D-11D2-945F-
00C04FB984F9},CN=Policies,CN=System,DC=example,DC=com
    1> displayName: Default Domain Policy;
>> Dn: CN={6AC1786C-016F-11D2-945F-
00C04fB984F9},CN=Policies,CN=System,DC=example,DC=com
    1> displayName: Default Domain Controllers Policy;

Chapter 7 – Controlling Returned Results

So far we have shown you how to retrieve information from the directory. The information is returned in an unordered sequence and this can sometimes make it very difficult to locate the details you are interested in. In some situations data will not be returned because it is hidden from standard queries or the result sets are too large. In this chapter we will examine ways of changing how information is returned and presented. We will look at controlling the visibility, size, order and format of the returned data.

Showing Deleted Objects

A standard LDAP search will not return objects in the Deleted Objects container. Before trying the example, create and then delete a user called Jill. Run the following query and you will find that no results are returned.

Set the Search dialog as follows:	
Base DN	dc=example,dc=com
Filter	(&(isDeleted=TRUE)(cn=jill*))
Scope	Subtree
Attributes	objectGUID

To retrieve these objects you need to use an LDAP control.

Open the Search Options dialog and click **Controls**, in the Controls dialog you need to check in the OID control that instructs the server to return deleted objects.

If you are using the version of LDP that comes with Microsoft® Windows® 2000 you will need to enter the OID **1.2.840.113556.1.4.417** into the **Object Identifier** field and then click **Check in>>**.

If you are using the Microsoft® Windows® Server 2003 version of LDP, in the Controls dialog select **Return Deleted Objects** from the **Load Predefined** drop-down list.

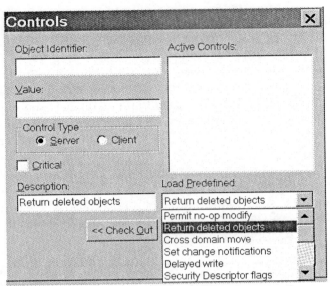

Figure 7.1 – Selecting a predefined control

Close the Controls dialog and in the Search Options dialog set the **Search Call Type** to **Extended** and the **Timeout** (s) to 120.

Run the previous search again and you will see the following results:

```
Getting 1 entries:
>> Dn: CN=Jill\0ADEL: 7e32d5aa-45de-779a-8764-
ac65789dd390,CN=Deleted Objects,DC=example,DC=com
        1> objectGUID: 7e32d5aa-45de-779a-8764-ac65789dd390;
```

Notice that the name of the object has been morphed; the common name and object GUID have been concatenated.

Many of the object's attributes are stripped when the object is deleted, if you want to see all the attributes with values that have been retained, set the search options attributes field to *. If you want a list of all the attributes that are retained on logical deletion you need to examine the *searchFlags* property defined for each attribute. See Search Flags and Matching Rules in Chapter 3.

Unknown SIDs

We mentioned tracking down "account unknown" issues in Chapter 5 and showed you this screenshot:

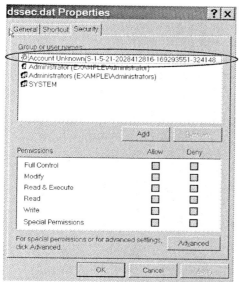

Figure 7.2 – Account unknown

Account unknown entries can appear because the account has been deleted. We have covered how to return deleted objects and now we are in a position to track down an unknown account entry.

So that you can try out the above scenario, create a Notepad document on an NTFS volume and set the security to allow John Full Control. Close the security dialogs. Now delete John's account object.

Check the security on the file and you will see the unknown account entry:

Account Unknown(S-1-5-21-2028412816-169293551-324148440-1140)

TIP: You could write down the number but we all know how tedious that is… Click **Advanced**, select the SID entry and click **Edit,** you can now copy the entry to the clipboard.

In the search dialog, paste in the SID.

Set the Search dialog as follows:	
Base DN	<SID=S-1-5-21-2028412816-169293551-324148440-1140>
Filter	(objectClass=*)
Scope	Base
Attributes	objectGUID;objectSID

Getting 1 entries:
>> Dn: CN=John\0ADEL:9d7de7a1-c835-44e1-8984-
464ac75e5509,CN=Deleted Objects,DC=example,DC=com
      1> objectGUID: 9d7de7a1-c835-44e1-8984-464ac75e5509;
      1> objectSid: S-1-5-21-2028412816-169293551-324148440-1140;

Managing Larger Sets of Results

The default buffer setting for LDP is 512 lines and 2048 characters per line.

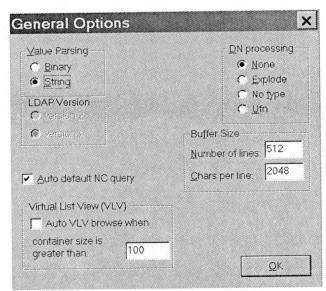

Figure 7.3 – General options

We recommend that you increase the number of lines to 4000; this will allow you to scroll back through large sets of results. You can leave the characters per line at the default setting. LDP will wrap lines to fit the size of the pane. Lines that are truncated because the 2048 character limit has been exceeded have an ellipsis appended. If you need to cram information onto the screen you could always change the font size using **View | Set Font**. Unfortunately you can only do this with the version of LDP supplied with Microsoft® Windows® Server 2003.

When you are about to receive a large set of results and you don't require the previous results, it is always worth remembering to clear the results pane using Ctrl + N. Once the data has been received you can use Ctrl + Home to jump to the top of the results and see how many values have been returned. When LDP displays "Getting 120 entries", 120 records are being returned. The records contain the distinguished name of an object plus any attributes that have been specified.

Retrieving over 1000 records

The maximum number of records that can be retrieved from the server in a single standard query is 1000. This value is set by the MaxPageSize LDAP policy value for the server. This value could be changed using ntdsutil.exe, however changing it could adversely affect server performance. To retrieve over 1000 records it is better to page the returned results. Paging will provide a faster response time to the first returned results and the search can be abandoned once the required data has been retrieved. If you are running Microsoft® Windows® Server 2003, Virtual List View provides an alternative to paging. See Virtual List View below.

Paging

Paging requires the use of an extended LDAP query which passes a control to the server. Paging is configured through the Options dialog. In this example we will set a very small page size so we can show you the beginning and end results of a paged query.

Set the Search dialog as follows:	
Base DN	dc=example,dc=com
Filter	(objectClass=*)
Scope	Subtree
Attributes	1.1

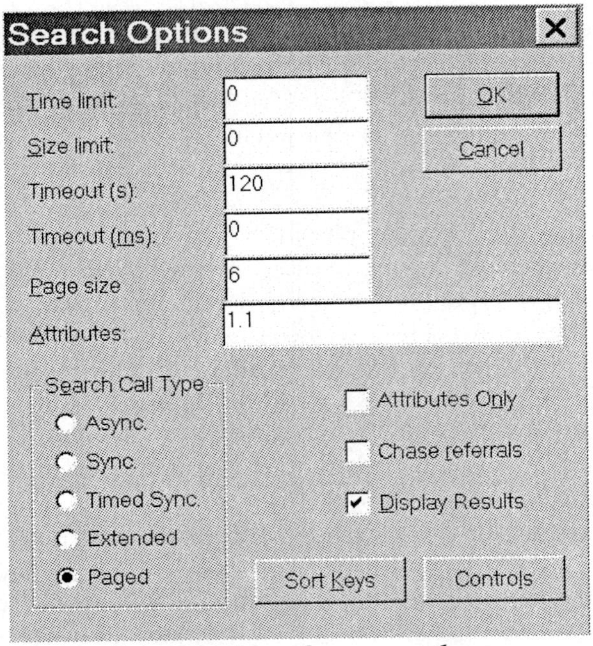

Figure 7.4 – Options for a paged query

```
Getting 6 entries:
>> Dn: DC=example,DC=com
>> Dn: CN=Users,DC=example,DC=com
>> Dn: CN=Computers,DC=example,DC=com
>> Dn: OU=Domain Controllers,DC=example,DC=com
>> Dn: CN=System,DC=example,DC=com
>> Dn: CN=LostAndFound,DC=example,DC=com
-----------
   -=>> 'Run' for more, 'Close' to abandon <<=-
```

You need to close and reopen the Search dialog before you can enter new search criteria.

The LDAP client passes the LDAP control 1.2.840.113556.1.4.319 to the server to instruct it to page the results. Using LDP and setting the paged option automatically passes the control to the server. You do not have to set a manual control through the Controls dialog.

Virtual List View (VLV)

VLV is implemented on Microsoft® Windows® Server 2003 and provides a mechanism to retrieve a portion of the results. The results are displayed in a list pane and from a user's perspective it appears as though you are simply scrolling through the results. In actual operation the client requests information from the server when required.

The results are alphabetically sorted and the server returns a portion of these results to fill the list view. The results returned are either based on an offset (scrollbar position) into the overall result set or are relative to a value that you specify for the sorted attribute.

The Virtual List View dialog is invoked with **View | Browse**. Enter the appropriate search criteria as you would in a normal Search dialog. The default sorted attribute is the common name.

In the Options dialog you need to set the timeout and the attributes to be returned.

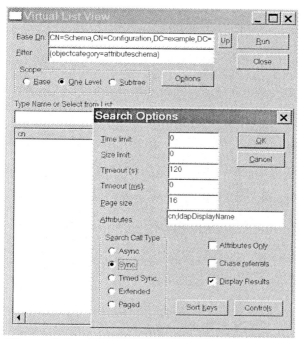

Figure 7.5 – Virtual list view options

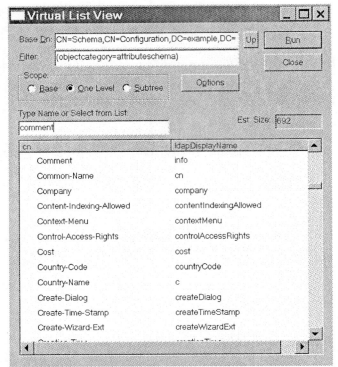

Figure 7.6 – VLV result set

The retrieved information is either controlled through the scrollbar or a value that you specify. In the above screenshot you can see the mappings between the common names of attributes and their LDAP display names. Notice the **Type Name or Select from List** field contains "comment" and the retrieved list is relative to this value. You will see that the LDAP display name for *comment* is *info*.

TIP: If you double click one of the entries in the list this becomes a suffix to the base DN. This allows you to further refine your search by drilling down into a subtree. To move back up through the tree, click **Up**.

To sort the list on a value other than the common name set a value via the Sort Keys dialog.

Open the Sort Keys dialog from the Search Options dialog. Enter the attribute name that you want to sort on and click **Check In>>**

To follow along with our example check in the *lDAPDisplayName*.

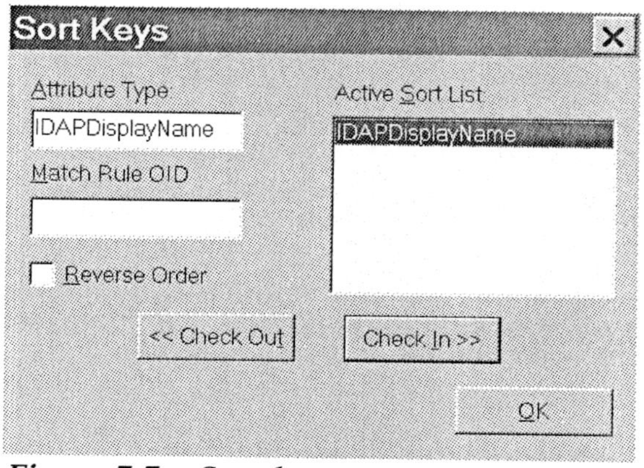

Figure 7.7 – Sort keys

Back in the Virtual List View dialog click **Run** and set the **Type Name or Select from List** field to *info*. You will now see that the list is sorted by *lDAPDisplayName*.

Sort Keys

The Sort Keys dialog is used to instruct the server to sort the returned results based on an attribute value. The dialog is invoked using **Browse | Search | Search Options | Sort Keys**.

The results returned from the LDAP search can be very detailed and confusing at times, sorting information can simplify understanding. Take as an example enumerating all linked attributes.

Enumerating linked attributes:

Set the Search dialog as follows:	
Base DN	cn=schema,cn=configuration,dc=example,dc=com
Filter	(&(objectCategory=attributeSchema)(LinkID=*))
Scope	One Level
Attributes	LinkID

We are only showing a sample of the overall set:

```
Getting 58 entries:
>> Dn: CN=Is-Member-Of-
DL,CN=Schema,CN=Configuration,DC=example,DC=com
        1> linkID: 3;
> Dn: CN=Is-Privilege-
Holder,CN=Schema,CN=Configuration,DC=example,DC=com
        1> linkID: 71;
>> Dn: CN=Managed-
By,CN=Schema,CN=Configuration,DC=example,DC=com
        1> linkID: 72;
>> Dn: CN=Managed-
Objects,CN=Schema,CN=Configuration,DC=example,DC=com
        1> linkID: 73;
>> Dn:
CN=Manager,CN=Schema,CN=Configuration,DC=example,DC=com
        1> linkID: 42;
>> Dn: CN=Mastered-
By,CN=Schema,CN=Configuration,DC=example,DC=com
        1> linkID: 77;
```

You will see that the results are in no particular order and it is difficult to locate the matching linked pairs. Remember forward-links have an even number for their *linkID* value and the associated back-link value is the forward-link value +1

To sort the list so that the values are in order, use the Sort Keys dialog and sort by *linkID* value.

Set the attribute name to *linkID* and click **Check In>>**

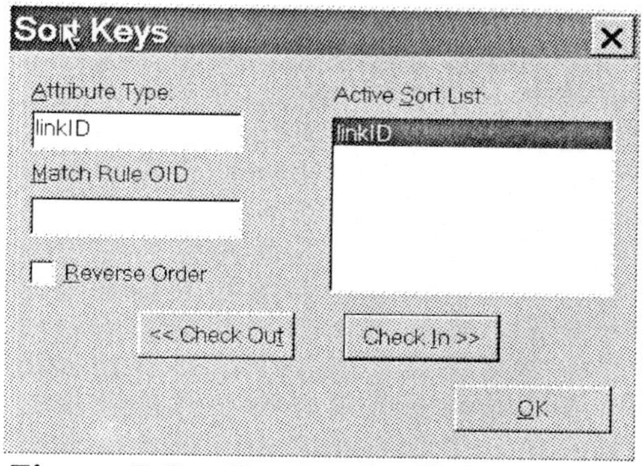

Figure 7.8 – Sorting by linkID

When you run the search, the LDAP client passes the LDAP control 1.2.840.113556.1.4.473 to the server to instruct it to sort the results. Before the sort will operate you must set the call type to **Extended** in the Search Options dialog.

We are only showing a sample of the overall set:

```
Getting 58 entries: (truncated)
>> Dn:
CN=Member,CN=Schema,CN=Configuration,DC=example,DC=com
        1> linkID: 2;
>> Dn: CN=Is-Member-Of-
DL,CN=Schema,CN=Configuration,DC=example,DC=com
        1> linkID: 3;
>> Dn:
CN=Manager,CN=Schema,CN=Configuration,DC=example,DC=com
        1> linkID: 42;
>> Dn:
CN=Reports,CN=Schema,CN=Configuration,DC=example,DC=com
        1> linkID: 43;
>> Dn:
CN=Owner,CN=Schema,CN=Configuration,DC=example,DC=com
```

Well that listing looks better, but if you have been reading through this chapter in order you are probably thinking "Why didn't we use VLV?". Well if we had Microsoft® Windows® Server 2003 we could have done!

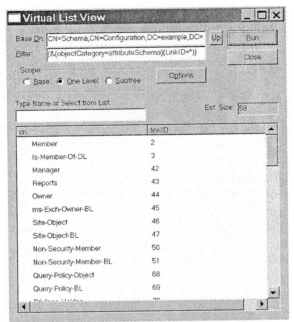

Figure 7.9 – Sort keys in virtual list view

Returning Search Statistics

In the Geek's Reference (Chapter 3) we discussed how the filter for an ANR search gets expanded by the server. We also mention the translation of the *objectCategory* value to a DN when you specify it using an LDAP display name. In this section we will look at retrieving Search Statistics which will show the filter expansion on Microsoft® Windows® Server 2003. The Search Statistics are retrieved using the Search Stats control (1.2.840.113556.1.4.970).

Open the Search Options dialog and click **Controls,** in the Controls dialog you need to check in the OID control that instructs the server to return the Search Stats.

If you are using the version of LDP that comes with Microsoft® Windows® 2000 you will need to enter the OID 1.2.840.113556.1.4.970 into the **Object Identifier** field and then click **Check in>>.** If you query a Microsoft® Windows® 2000 Server it will provide you with limited statistics, it does not show the filter expansion.

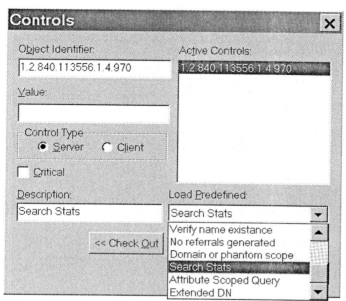

Figure 7.10 – Setting a predefined control

Close the Controls dialog and in the Search Options dialog set the **Search Call Type** to **Extended** and the **Timeout** (s) to 120.

To see the ANR filter expansion:

Set the Search dialog as follows:	
Base DN	dc=example,dc=com
Filter	(ANR=sally)
Scope	Subtree
Attributes	1.1

```
        Used Filter:
( | (displayName=sally*)  (givenName=sally*)
(legacyExchangeDN=sally)  (msDS-
AdditionalSamAccountName=sally*)
(physicalDeliveryOfficeName=sally*)
(proxyAddresses=sally*)  (name=sally*)  (sAMAccountName=sally*)
(sn=sally*) )
        Used Indexes:
idx_sn:9:N;idx_sAMAccountName:8:N;idx_name:7:P;
idx_proxyAddresses:6:N;idx_physicalDeliveryOfficeName:5:N;
idx_msDSAdditionalSamAccountName:4:N;idx_legacyExchangeDN:3:N;
idx_givenName:2:N;idx_displayName:1:N;
```

Notice that the search statistics also show you which indexes were used.

To see the *objectCategory* name expansion:

Set the Search dialog as follows:	
Base DN	dc=example,dc=com
Filter	(objectCategory=user)
Scope	Subtree
Attributes	1.1

```
        Used Filter:
(objectCategory=CN=Person,CN=Schema,CN=Configuration,
DC=example,DC=com)
        Used Indexes:
PDNT_index:19:N;
```

Other Ways of Presenting Data

LDP offers a number of ways of presenting and interpreting data and these are summed up in this section.

Open the General Options dialog via **Options | General** and you will find two options for changing the data format:

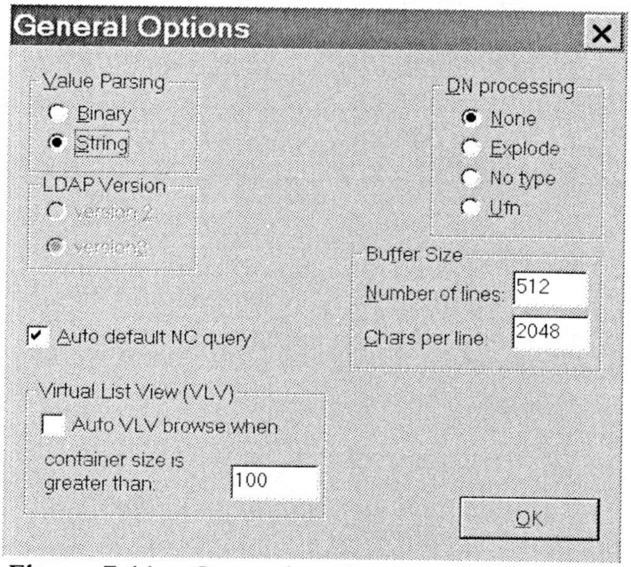

Figure 7.11 – General options

DN Processing

DN processing converts the way in which the distinguished names are displayed in the results window. This includes various combinations of commas, semi-colons and spaces.

None – comma separated, no spaces
>   Dn: cn=Users,dc=example,dc=com,

Explode – semi-colon separated, spaces
>   Dn: cn=Users; dc=example; dc=com;

No type – semi-colon separated, spaces, no cn= or dc=
>   Dn: Users; example; com;

Ufn (User Friendly Name) – comma separated, spaces
>   Dn: cn=Users, dc=example, dc=com,

Value Parsing

Where ever possible LDP will convert the LDAP native format to ASCII characters to make it readable. Where the string conversion cannot be performed, the results can be displayed in binary.

For example you can request the access control list for an object:

Set the Search dialog as follows:	
Base DN	ou=england,dc=example,dc=com
Filter	(objectCategory=*)
Scope	Base
Attributes	NTSecurityDescriptor

```
Matched DNs:
Getting 1 entries:
>> Dn: OU=England,DC=example,DC=com
nTSecurityDescriptor: <LDP: Binary blob>
```

As you will see this is shown as being a binary blob. Set the **Value Parsing** option to **Binary** and rerun the query:

```
Getting 1 entries: (truncated)
>> Dn: OU=England,DC=example,DC=com
1> nTSecurityDescriptor:
01 00 14 8c a8 05 00 00 c4 05 00 00 14 00 00 00    ...Œ¨...Ä.......
8c 00 00 00 04 00 78 00 02 00 00 00 07 52 38 00    Œ.....x......R8.
20 00 00 00 03 00 00 00 be 3b 0e f3 f0 9f d1 11    ......¾;.óðŸÑ.
b6 03 00 00 f8 03 67 c1 a5 7a 96 bf e6 0d d0 11    ¶...ø.gÁ¥z–¿æ.Ð.
a2 85 00 aa 00 30 49 e2 01 01 00 00 00 00 00 01    ¢....ª.0Iâ........
00 00 00 00 07 52 38 00 20 00 00 00 03 00 00 00    .....R8. .......
```

Viewing the Security Descriptor

Well we've now got the results but perhaps not too meaningful! Luckily LDP offers an option to translate the ACL. Before carrying out any further commands switch the **Value Parsing** back to **String**.

Select **Browse | Security | Security Descriptor** and set the DN to the England OU. We have reduced and truncated these results.

```
Getting 1 entries:
>> Dn: OU=England,DC=example,DC=com
nTSecurityDescriptor:

Security Descriptor:SD Revision: 1
SD Control:  0x8c04
              SE_DACL_PRESENT
              SE_DACL_AUTO_INHERITED
              SE_SACL_AUTO_INHERITED
              SE_SELF_RELATIVE
Owner: EXAMPLE\Domain Admins S-1-5-21-2028412816-169293551-
324148440-512
Group: EXAMPLE\Domain Users S-1-5-21-2028412816-169293551-
324148440-513
DACL:
      Revision     4
      Size:        1308 bytes
      # Aces:      28
      Ace[0]
      Ace Type:  0x0 - ACCESS_ALLOWED_ACE_TYPE
      Ace Size:  20 bytes
      Ace Flags: 0x0
      Ace Mask:  0x000f01ff
                  DELETE
                  READ_CONTROL
```

Replication Metadata

LDP will translate the replication metadata for an object. Each object has an overall USN changed value and all of the individual attributes have an associated USN local value. The metadata for the attributes is held in the *replPropertyMetaData* attribute for the object in a compressed binary format.

Use the **Browse | Replication | View Metadata** and set the DN to the England OU:

Getting 'ou=england,dc=example,dc=com' metadata...
7 entries.

AttID	Ver	Loc.USN	Originating DSA	Org.USN	Org.Time/Date
0	1	15451	ecaf8b37-bfcc–4b91–804c-de45e6cb1b80	15451	2002-08-30 06:50:26
b	1	15451	ecaf8b37-bfcc–4b91–804c-de45e6cb1b80	15451	2002-08-30 06:50:26
20001	1	15451	ecaf8b37-bfcc–4b91–804c-de45e6cb1b80	15451	2002-08-30 06:50:26
20002	1	15451	ecaf8b37-bfcc–4b91–804c-de45e6cb1b80	15451	2002-08-30 06:50:26
20119	1	15451	ecaf8b37-bfcc–4b91–804c-de45e6cb1b80	15451	2002-08-30 06:50:26
90001	1	15451	ecaf8b37-bfcc–4b91–804c-de45e6cb1b80	15451	2002-08-30 06:50:26
9030e	1	15451	ecaf8b37-bfcc–4b91–804c-de45e6cb1b80	15451	2002-08-30 06:50:26

Unfortunately the Attribute ID (*AttID*) does not easily identify the attribute names. This value represents the attribute OID, however because of an optimisation in the directory the full OID string is not used. There are hundreds of OIDs used in the AD and many of the OIDs start with the same dotted strings. To optimise access they are be grouped by prefix. The Attribute ID consists of an OID prefix identifier combined with the last digits of the actual OID.

In the above example 0 refers to **2.5.4.0** which identifies the *objectClass* and b refers to **2.5.4.11** which identifies the organization unit name (OU).

Although you can use LDP to recover this information we prefer to use the command line tool repadmin.exe

```
C:\>repadmin /showmeta ou=england,dc=example,dc=com

7 entries.
Loc.USN            Originating DC        Org.USN Org.Time/Date      Ver Attribute
=======            ===============       ======= ==============     === ==========
15451              London\NETADS01-RC1   15451 2002-08-30 06:50:26  1 objectCategory
15451              London\NETADS01-RC1   15451 2002-08-30 06:50:26  1 name
15451              London\NETADS01-RC1   15451 2002-08-30 06:50:26  1 nTSecurityDescriptor
15451              London\NETADS01-RC1   15451 2002-08-30 06:50:26  1 whenCreated
15451              London\NETADS01-RC1   15451 2002-08-30 06:50:26  1 instanceType
15451              London\NETADS01-RC1   15451 2002-08-30 06:50:26  1 ou
15451              London\NETADS01-RC1   15451 2002-08-30 06:50:26  1 objectClass
```

Chapter 8 – Manipulating Objects and Attributes

Making Changes

If you are going to make changes to the directory always use the most appropriate tools. For instance if you are creating a normal user, you should not create the user using LDP. However while maintaining your systems there will be times when you need to manipulate an object or attribute and there is no associated user interface. So what are your options? You could programmatically make changes, but hey, who wants to write code when you've got great tools such as LDP.

In this chapter we will show you how to use LDP to add, modify, compare and delete objects and attribute values. In order to aid understanding, we will make these additions and changes to objects with which you are familiar such as users and OUs.

Adding New Objects into the Directory

When a new object is added to the directory the mandatory attributes defined for that object must be populated, for details see Creating Objects in Chapter 3.

Objects are added to the directory using LDP via the Add dialog. Open the dialog using **Browse | Add Child**. You will need to define the distinguished name of the new object to be created and also set all of the required mandatory attributes.

Use Schema Manager to view the mandatory attributes associated with an object.

Creating a User Account Object

In our first example we will show you how to create a user object. Open Schema Manager, drilldown to the user class definition and select the **Type** column to view the mandatory attributes required to create a user object.

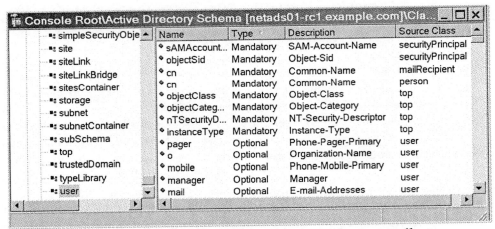

Figure 8.1 – Schema Manager showing user mandatory attributes

Schema manager shows seven mandatory attributes required for a user:

- *sAMAccountName*
- *objectSID*
- *cn*
- *objectClass*
- *objectCategory*
- *nTSecurityDescriptor*
- *instanceType*

On Microsoft® Windows® Server 2003, the only two attributes that you must set are *cn* and *objectClass,* the system will create the rest of the values. In Microsoft® Windows® 2000 you will also need to create a *sAMAccountName.*

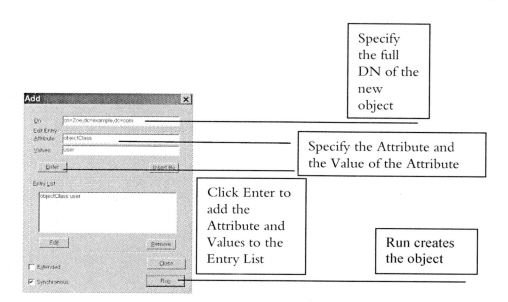

Figure 8.2 – Adding a user object with minimum attributes

The **Insert file** key allows you to import the attribute's value from a file. This could be useful for entering binary data.

Zoe

Figure 8.3 – New user object

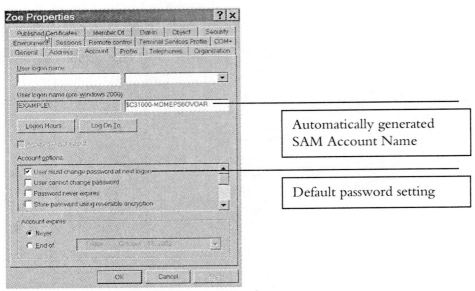

Figure 8.4 – New user object properties

As you will see the account is disabled, it has no user principal name and a rather tricky SAM account name. When you create a user account object or any other type of object you will invariably want to set more than just the mandatory attributes. Delete Zoe in Active Directory® Users and Computers.

The *userAccountControl* attribute defines characteristics for the account and the flags are documented in Apendix E, *userAccountControl* Flags. The *pwdLastSet* attribute disables the need for the user to change password at first logon.

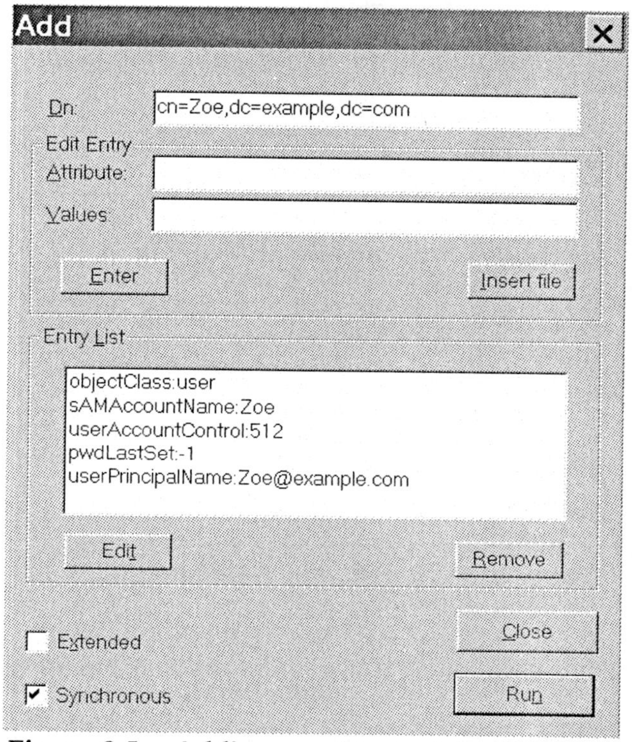

Add ✕

Dn: cn=Zoe,dc=example,dc=com

Edit Entry
Attribute:
Values:

Enter   Insert file

Entry List

objectClass:user
sAMAccountName:Zoe
userAccountControl:512
pwdLastSet:-1
userPrincipalName:Zoe@example.com

Edit   Remove

☐ Extended   Close

☑ Synchronous   Run

Figure 8.5 – Adding an object with additional attributes

Zoe

Figure 8.6 – New user object

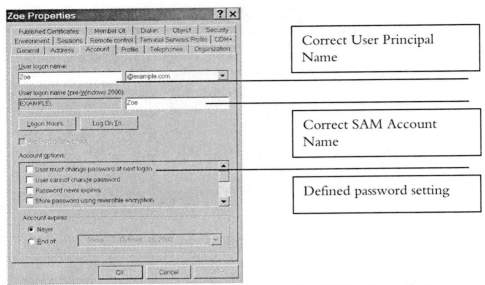

Figure 8.7 – New user object properties with additional attributes

Creating a New OU

In our second example we will create a new OU. By now you should know the process:

      – Identify the mandatory attributes via Schema Manager
      – Work out which of those attributes the system can probably set
      – Create the object and set the remaining attributes

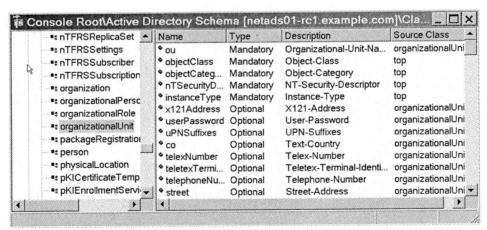

Figure 8.8 – OU mandatory attributes

As you can see you only have to set the name (*ou*) and the *objectClass*. The relative distinguished name for an OU is stored in its *ou* attribute, for more details see Object Names in Chapter 3.

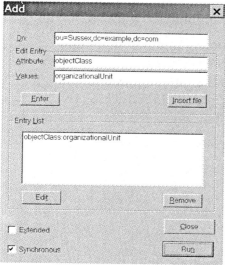

Figure 8.9 – Adding an OU

Modifying Attributes

You can add, delete and replace attributes using the Modify dialog. Using this LDP command it is possible to modify both single-valued and multi-valued attributes. If you are not sure of the attributes LDAP display name, look it up in Schema Manager.

You need to enter the distinguished name of the object before you can modify any of its attributes. When modifying attributes there are three options, Add, Delete and Replace. These options behave differently depending on whether you are modifying single-valued or multi-valued attributes.

Single-Valued Attributes

Option	Specified	Result
Add	Attribute name and value	Sets the value of the specified attribute. Can only be used if the current value is not set
Delete	Attribute name	Clears the specified attribute
Replace	Attribute name and value	Replaces the current value with the new value

Multi-Valued Attributes

Option	Specify	Result
Add	Attribute name and value	Adds the specified value to the current values already set for the attribute. If the attribute is currently not set then the first value is added
Delete	Attribute name	Clears the specified attribute
Delete	Attribute name and value	Deletes the specified value from the multi-valued attribute
Replace	Attribute name and value	Replaces all of the current values with the new value

Modifying a Single-Valued Attribute

As an example we are going to add a description for John. (If you are following the examples in the book, you will have deleted John in Chapter 7. Recreate John's user object prior to performing this example.) Firstly, use **Browse | Search** to confirm the current value of the description attribute:

Set the Search dialog as follows:	
Base DN	cn=john,ou=london,ou=england,dc=example,dc=com
Filter	(objectClass=*)
Scope	Base
Attributes	Description

```
Matched DNs:
Getting 1 entries:
>> Dn: CN=John,OU=London,OU=England,DC=example,DC=com
```

John doesn't have a description, so no description attribute was returned. Remember the search will only return populated attributes.

To change the description, select **Browse | Modify**.

Set the Modify dialog as follows:	
Base DN	cn=john,ou=london,ou=england,dc=example,dc=com
Attribute:	Description
Values	Great Geek

Select the **Add** radio button. Description is a single-valued attribute, the modification will fail if you try to add a new description when one already exists.

Click **Enter** to move the instruction into the **Entry List**.

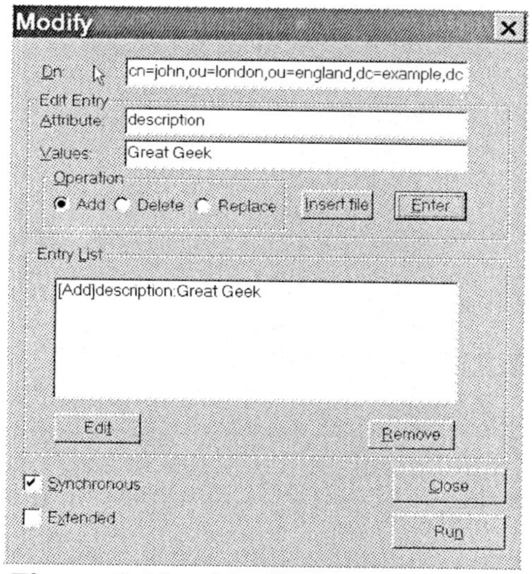

Figure 8.10 – Modifying a user object

Click **Run** to trigger an LDAP request to update the Active Directory®.

The results pane will confirm the modification although it will not list the specific changes.

```
***Call Modify...
ldap_modify_s(ld,
'cn=john,ou=london,ou=england,dc=example,dc=com',[1] attrs);

Modified "cn=john,ou=london,ou=england,dc=example,dc=com".
```

Click **Run** again and you will get the following result because now the attribute value is already set.

```
***Call Modify...
ldap_modify_s(ld,
'cn=john,ou=london,ou=england,dc=example,dc=com',[1] attrs);
Error: Modify: Attribute Or Value Exists. <20>
```

Run **Browse | Search** to confirm the change.

Modifying Multi-Valued Attributes

The distinguished names of members of a group are stored in the group object's *member* attribute, this is a multi-valued attribute. In this next example you will change the values held in the *member* attribute of our group object:

cn=sales,ou=england, dc=example,dc=com

You can add multiple values to a multi-valued attribute in a single operation.

Set the Modify dialog as follows:	
Base DN	cn=sales,ou=england,dc=example,dc=com
Attribute:	member

Values	Enter the values together, with each DN separated by a semicolon:
	 cn=sally,ou=London,ou=england,dc=example,dc=com;
	 cn=john, ou=London,ou=england,dc=example,dc=com;
	 cn=fred,ou=UK,dc=child,dc=example,dc=com

Select the **Add** radio button.

Click **Enter** to move the instruction into the **Entry List**.

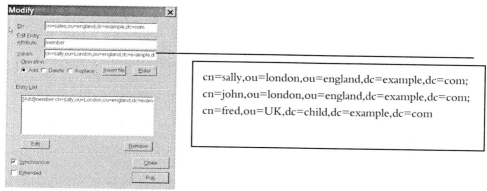

cn=sally,ou=london,ou=england,dc=example,dc=com;
cn=john,ou=london,ou=england,dc=example,dc=com;
cn=fred,ou=UK,dc=child,dc=example,dc=com

Figure 8.11 – Modifying a multi-valued attribute

Click **Run** to trigger an LDAP request to update the Active Directory®.

The results pane will show confirmation of the modification although it will not list the specific changes.

```
***Call Modify...
ldap_modify_s(ld, 'cn=sales,ou=england,dc=example,dc=com',[1] attrs);
Modified "cn=sales,ou=england,dc=example,dc=com".
```

Use the LDP **Search** dialog to display the members of the group.

Set the Search dialog as follows:	
Base DN	cn=sales,ou=england,dc=example,dc=com
Filter	(objectClass=*)
Scope	Base
Set the Search Options dialog as follows:	
Attributes	member

```
Getting 1 entries:
>> Dn: cn=sales,ou=england,dc=example,dc=com
      3>member:
CN=Sally,OU=London,OU=England,DC=example,DC=com;
CN=John,OU=London,OU=England,DC=example,DC=com;
CN=Fred,OU=UK,DC=child,DC=example,DC=com;
```

You can test out the following scenarios. Remember to set the DN for the group object, set the attribute field to *member*, the appropriate attribute value and click **Enter** to load the **Entry List**.

- — If you select **Delete** and specify the DN for a contained user, just that user is removed from the *member* attribute.
- — If you select **Delete** without specifying a value, all the members will be deleted.
- — If you select **Add** you can add further members to the list
- — If you select **Replace** all the previous values are replaced with the new value

Modifying a Distinguished Name

Using **Browse | Modify DN** you can change the distinguished name of an object.

If you just want to change the name used to identify the object, change the object's relative distinguished name. If you want to move the object, change one or more of the object's path names.

For example, to move John from the London OU to England OU:

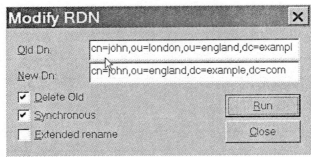

Figure 8.12 – Modify DN

As an example of moving and renaming the London OU:

Set the Modify DN dialog as follows:	
Old DN:	ou=london,ou=england,dc=example,dc=com
New DN:	ou=paris,dc=example,dc=com

This will rename the London OU to Paris and move it to the root of the example.com domain.

You can only uncheck the **Delete Old** box if doing so would not cause a conflict within the directory. As the objects we are working with are identified by GUID, you would not be able to make a copy to anywhere else in the directory without this conflict. An *objectClass* that has no GUID or other unique identifier would not be subject to this caveat.

Comparing Attribute Values

Using Compare, you compare the set value of an object's attribute with a specified value. The result returned is either TRUE or FALSE. If the value is not set, you will receive a "No Such Attribute" error message. Invoke the **Compare** dialog using **Browse | Compare**

As an example you can test if the description attribute of the Sales OU is set to "UK Sales"

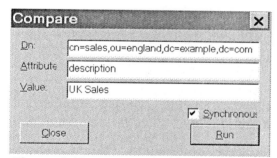

Figure 8.13 – Comparing an attribute value

```
ldap_compare_s(0x8022c8,
"cn=sales,ou=england,dc=example,dc=com", "description", "UK Sales")
Results: TRUE. <6>
```

Deleting Objects using the Microsoft® Windows® 2000 version of LDP

In the version of LDP that comes with Microsoft® Windows® 2000 you can only use this feature for leaf objects – that is an object that has no children. So if you wanted to delete an OU, you would have to delete all the contained objects first. Here is an example of deleting a user object:

Set the Delete dialog as follows:	
DN:	cn=john,ou=england,dc=example,dc=com
Select	Synchronous

You will not receive any warning or "are you sure" type dialogs before the deletion takes place. Be careful☺.

The results pane will confirm the deletion

```
ldap_delete_s(ld, " cn=john,ou=england,dc=example,dc=com ");
Deleted " cn=john,ou=england,dc=example,dc=com "
```

If the object you are attempting to delete has contained users, you will receive the following error message:

```
ldap_delete_s(ld, "ou=england,dc=example,dc=com");
Error: Delete: Not allowed on Non-leaf. <66>
```

Deleting Objects using the Microsoft® Windows® Server 2003 version of LDP

There is now the ability to delete all objects within a container in a single command. The selection of **Recursive (client)** sends the appropriate control to achieve this. We will delete the England OU and its contents in the following example.

Set the Delete dialog as follows:	
DN:	ou=england,dc=example,dc=com
Select	Synchronous
Select	Recursive (Client)

The results pane will show confirmation of the deletion

```
deleting "ou=england,dc=example,dc=com"...
        deleted 2 entries
```

Chapter 9 – A Different Way of Seeing and Doing Things

Viewing the Entire Directory Tree

If you have followed through the rest of this book, you can now enumerate, sort and find the data you require. To do this you need to establish the appropriate search criteria by setting the filter, base DN and scope. LDP allows you to browse naming contexts via a tree view.

The tree view is useful for quickly locating information. If you need to find specific information about a number of attributes or objects, we would encourage you to use the standard LDP search. The search provides a clear results page presenting just the information you have requested. The tree view will require you to individually examine objects and the results can be cluttered and confusing.

Combinations can always be good! Drill down through the directory in the tree view and select a particular container or object. If you right-click the node and open the Search dialog the base DN is already populated with the DN of the selected node.

Tree View

Using **View | Tree** you can specify the base object for the left hand side scope pane. By default, the field is blank and no objects are listed. Specify your base DN in the dialog, navigate through the Directory Information Tree and identify a starting point for your activities. When you double-click your chosen node, two things will happen:

- All populated attributes for that object will be enumerated in the right hand results pane
- The left pane will display any contained objects

Most of the functions that are available through the main **Browse** menu are available on the right-click context menu in the tree view.

In this example we will drill-down into our child.example.com domain and work with our user Fred.

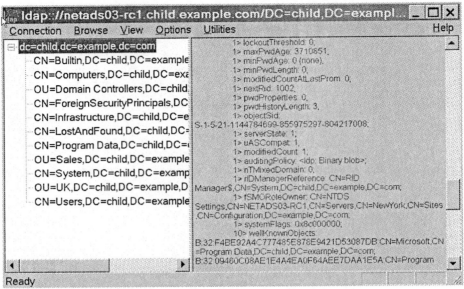

Figure 9.1 – Tree view

Moving an Object in Tree View

To move Fred from the UK OU to the root of the child domain, select Fred from your tree view. Right-click to open the context menu and select Modify DN. This invokes the Modify DN dialog that you have seen previously in Chapter 8. The advantage of using tree view is that the DN is already populated.

TIP: You can use **Modify DN** to move objects between containers, although in Microsoft® Windows® Server 2003 Active Directory® Users and Computers the new drag and drop feature might be somewhat faster!

Set the Modify DN dialog as follows:	
Old DN:	cn=Fred,ou=UK,dc=child,dc=example,dc=com
New DN:	cn=Fred,dc=child,dc=example,dc=com

```
0x0 = ldap_modrdn2_s(ld,
CN=Fred,OU=UK,DC=child,DC=example,DC=com,
CN=Fred,DC=child,DC=example,DC=com, TRUE)
Rdn "CN=Fred,OU=UK,DC=child,DC=example,DC=com" modified to
"CN=Fred,DC=child,DC=example,DC=com"
```

Deleting an OU and it's Contained Objects Through Tree view

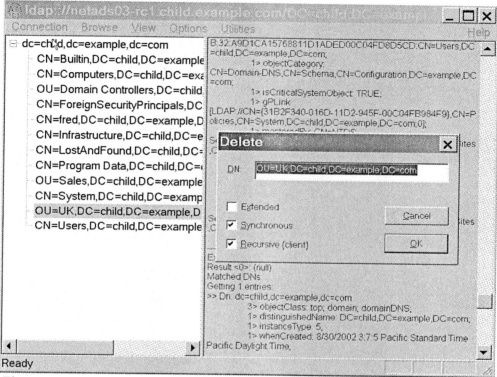

Figure 9.2 – Deleting an OU through the tree view

Right click the UK OU, select **Delete**. To delete any contained objects along with the container, select **Recursive (client)** and select **OK**.

The results set will display

```
deleting "OU=UK,DC=child,DC=example,DC=com"...
        deleted 1 entries
```

Viewing Your Live Enterprise Tree

To see a graphical display of the domain controllers and domains in the enterprise tree, select **Browse | Enterprise Configuration**. This will display your tree and detail server names. Offline domain controllers are indicated with a red cross.

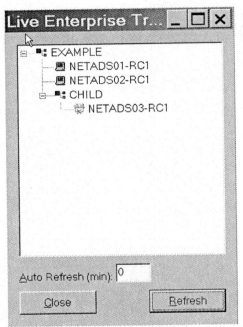

Figure 9.3 – Live enterprise tree view

Chapter 10 – Tips on Creating Efficient Searches

You should observe a number of guidelines in order to create efficient searches within the directory. In a small directory an inefficient search will have little impact, but on larger directories the impact can be significant.

Restrict the search scope

Don't search the whole directory if you know the location of the object or the subtree that it is in.

Indexed attributes should be used wherever possible

When defining a query filter at least one attribute should be indexed. For example use:

$$(\&(objectCategory=user)(description=production\star))$$

rather than:

$$(\&(objectClass=user)(description=production\star))$$

objectClass is not indexed and is multi-valued.

Limit the number of attributes returned

Set the options so that only the attributes you require are returned. If you only require the distinguished names of the objects set the attribute field to the 1.1 OID.

Limit the use of Ambiguous Name Resolution

If you use multiple ANR searches within the same filter, this will be expanded by the server to an extremely large filter. Restrict the filter to using a single ANR search. For example, don't use:

$$(|(anr=john)(anr=lena)(anr=james)(anr=kit)))$$

Consider medial searches

Medial searches of the form (attribute=$\star$th) or (attribute=$\star$th$\star$) are very inefficient in Microsoft® Windows® 2000 and should be avoided. If it is required to perform medial searches on Microsoft® Windows® Server 2003, it is important to make sure that the specified attribute has a medial index. This is enabled through the *searchFlags* property of the attribute.

AND and OR operators

The placement of operators can improve search performance as the query processor can take advantage of index intersections. Place AND operators inside nested filters. For example, the following two filters achieve the same result but the second one is more efficient:

(&(expression A)(|(expression B)(expression C)))
(|(&(expression A)(expression B))(&(expression A)(expression C)))

Avoid redundant operators

The following two filters achieve the same result but the second one is more efficient:

(&(expression A)(&(expression B)(expression C)))
(&(expression A)(expression B)(expression C))

Bitwise AND and OR matching rules

Use these only when required as they impact on performance. Indexes cannot be used for the matching rule as each value has to be tested. Set up a filter to combine a matching rule with an indexed attribute.

NOT operator may return undesired results

The NOT operator can be used to search for values that are not set. As an example you could use the filter (!(employeeNumber>=123)) to return all objects that do not have an *employeeNumber* greater than or equal to 123. The problem with this NOT operator is that the filter will also evaluate TRUE if

- The attribute is not set
- Security settings do not allow access to the attribute.

To avoid these problems you should rewrite the filter as:

(employeeNumber<=122)

Appendix A – Test Forest Configuration

All of our examples have been run against our test forest, the forest consists of two domains. In addition to the default users and containers, we have added three organisational units, three users and one security group. It is these additional objects that we will work with in our examples.

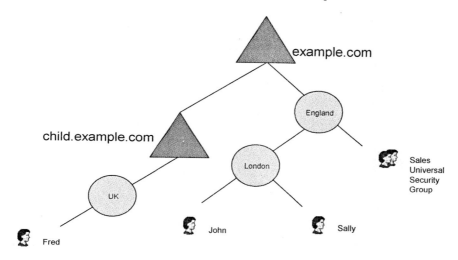

Figure A.1 – Test forest configuration

Our DC's are named NETADS01-RC1 for the DC in example.com and NETADS03-RC1 for the DC in child.example.com. These names are not important for the examples. We created this environment using the scripts below:

SCRIPT 1: Run on DC in example.com domain

```
Const ADS_GROUP_TYPE_UNIVERSAL_GROUP = &H8
Const ADS_GROUP_TYPE_SECURITY_ENABLED = &H80000000

'Set path to root of directory
        ADpath = "LDAP://dc=example,dc=com"
        Set objAD = GetObject(ADpath)
        Set objOU = objAD.Create("OrganizationalUnit", "ou=England")
'Update the DS
        objOU.SetInfo
'Set description
        objOU.Description = "Great Country"
        objOU.SetInfo
'Set path to England OU
        ADpath = "LDAP://ou=England,dc=example,dc=com"
        Set objAD = GetObject(ADpath)
'Create our universal group
        Set objUGrp = objAD.Create("group", "cn=Sales")
        objUGrp.samAccountName = "Sales"
        objUGrp.Description = "UK Sales"
        objUGrp.groupType = ADS_GROUP_TYPE_UNIVERSAL_GROUP or ADS_GROUP_TYPE_SECURITY_ENABLED
        objUGrp.SetInfo
'Create London OU
        Set objOU = objAD.Create("OrganizationalUnit", "ou=London")
'Update the DS
        objOU.SetInfo
'Set description
        objOU.Description = "Great City"
        objOU.SetInfo
'Create 1 user with the name Sally
        name = "Sally"
        Set objUser = objOU.Create("user", "cn=" & name)
'Set the properties of the new user
        objUser.samAccountName = name
        objUser.userPrincipalName = name
'Add account to DS
        objUser.SetInfo
'Set account properties
        objUser.AccountDisabled = FALSE
        objUser.pwdLastSet = -1
        objUser.Description = "Great Lady"
        objUser.SetInfo
'Create 1 user with the name John
        name = "John"
        Set objUser = objOU.Create("user", "cn=" & name)
'Set the properties of the new user
        objUser.samAccountName = name
        objUser.userPrincipalName = name
'Add account to DS
        objUser.SetInfo
'Set account properties
        objUser.AccountDisabled = FALSE
        objUser.pwdLastSet = -1
        objUser.SetInfo

WScript.Echo "All Done"
```

SCRIPT 2: Run on a DC in child.example.com domain

```
'Set path to root of directory
        ADpath = "LDAP://dc=child,dc=example,dc=com"
        Set objAD = GetObject(ADpath)
        Set objOU = objAD.Create("OrganizationalUnit", "ou=UK")
'Update the DS
        objOU.SetInfo
'Set description
        objOU.Description = "Great Place"
        objOU.SetInfo
'Create 1 user with the name Fred
        name = "Fred"
        Set objUser = objOU.Create("user", "cn=" & name)
'Set the properties of the new user
        objUser.samAccountName = name
        objUser.userPrincipalName = name
'Add account to DS
        objUser.SetInfo
'Set account properties
        objUser.AccountDisabled = FALSE
        objUser.pwdLastSet = -1
        objUser.Description = "Great Dancer"
        objUser.SetInfo
WScript.Echo "All Done"
```

Setting the Initial Search Conditions

We want your trial searches to work and we're sure you want the same, we highly recommend that your copy of LDP is configured in the same way as ours.

Open the Search Options dialog (**Browse | Search | Options**) and configure the settings as follows:

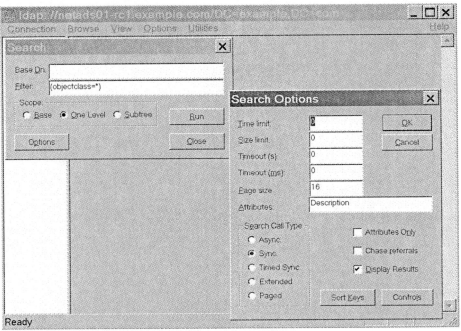

Figure A.2 – Test forest search options dialog

Click on the Sort Keys button and make sure that all the fields in the Sort Keys dialog are blank. If any values appear in the **Active Sort List** field remove them by clicking **<<Check Out**.

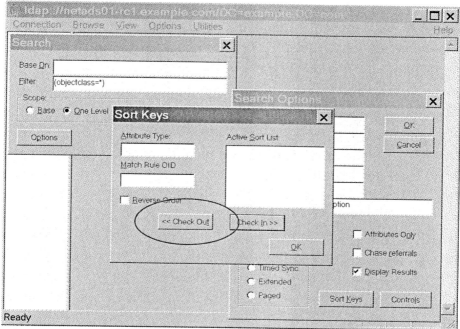

Figure A.3 – Test forest sort keys dialog

Close the Sort Key dialog and go into the Controls dialog box. Check out any active controls.

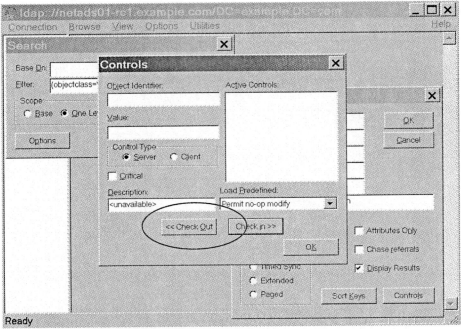

Figure A.4 – Test forest controls dialog

Appendix B – UI Text Strings
User Object UI Text Names Mapped to Attribute LDAP Display Names for US-English (409) Locale

The display specifier defines the relationship between the text strings used to identify the attribute values displayed in the user interface and the LDAP display names of the attributes that store data. This relationship is defined in the multi-valued *attributeDisplayNames* attribute.

To export the mappings between the user object UI text names and the attribute LDAP display names, we created a script that returns the *atributeDisplayNames* value for the display specifier associated with user objects. The file can be manipulated with a CSV editor such as Microsoft® Excel®.

The command string must be on a single line:

```
csvde -f details.csv -d "cn=user-
display,cn=409,cn=displaySpecifiers,cn=configuration,dc=example,dc=
com" -r "(objectClass=*)"  -l "attributeDisplayNames"
```

Some of the mappings are obvious:

UI text name	LDAP Display Names
Direct Reports	directReports
Description	description
Department	department
Company	company
Comment	comment

Others are less obvious:

UI text name	LDAP Display Names
Country Abbreviation	c
Name	cn
Country	co
X500 Distinguished Name	distinguishedName
Fax Number	facsimileTelephoneNumber
Generational Suffix	generationQualifier
First Name	givenName
Home Folder	homeDirectory
Home Address	homePostalAddress
Notes	info
International ISDN Number (Others)	internationalISDNNumber
IP Phone Number	ipPhone
City	l
E-Mail Address	mail
Mobile Number	mobile
Fax Number (Others)	otherFacsimileTelephoneNumber
Home Phone Number (Others)	otherHomePhone
IP Phone Number (Others)	otherIpPhone
E-Mail Address (Others)	otherMailbox
Mobile Number (Others)	otherMobile
Pager Number (Others)	otherPager
Phone Number (Others)	otherTelephone
Pager Number	pager
Title	personalTitle
Office Location	physicalDeliveryOfficeName
ZIP/Postal Code	postalCode
International ISDN Number	primaryInternationalISDNNumber
Telex Number	primaryTelexNumber
Logon Name (pre-Windows 2000)	samAccountName
Last Name	sn
State/Province	st
Job Title	title
Web Page Address (Others)	url
Logon Name	userPrincipalName
Logon Workstations	userWorkstations
Web Page Address	wWWHomePage

Appendix C – Object Names
LDAP Display Names mapped to Common Names

One of the simplest ways of converting an individual LDAP display name to its associated common name is to use Schema Manager. Schema Manager organizes attributes and objects by their LDAP display names. Select the appropriate name and open the property dialog to display the common name.

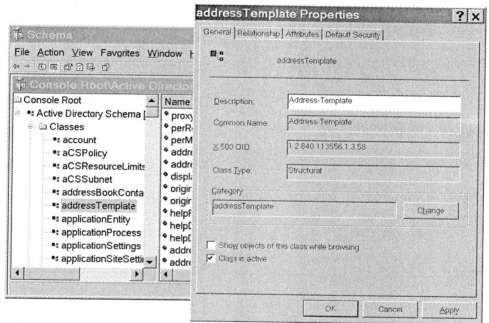

Figure C.1 – Object LDAP display name to common name mapping

You can map between the names using LDP, order the data using Sort Keys or Virtual List View.

To create this documentation we used csvde.exe to export the mappings between the object common names and the object LDAP display names. We created a script that returns the DN, the CN and the LDAP display name into a comma separated file. The file can be manipulated with a CSV editor such as Microsoft® Excel®.

The command string must be on a single line:

```
csvde -f details.csv -d
"cn=schema,cn=configuration,dc=example,dc=com"
-r "(objectClass=classSchema)"  -l "cn,lDAPDisplayName"
pause
```

Name Mapping

The mapping between LDAP display names and common names is fairly obvious and mainly involves the addition of a hyphen or two. The LDAP display name drops the initial capital letter and concatenates the words preserving the remaining capitalization. There are less than 200 object names returned when the script is run on Microsoft® Windows® Server 2003.

This is a small extract from the result set that the script produced:

LDAP Display Names	Common Names
organizationalPerson	Organizational-Person
organizationalRole	Organizational-Role
organizationalUnit	Organizational-Unit
packageRegistration	Package-Registration
person	Person
physicalLocation	Physical-Location

Appendix D – Attribute Names
LDAP Display Names mapped to Common Names

One of the simplest ways of converting an individual LDAP display name to its associated common name is to use Schema Manager. Schema Manager organizes attributes and objects by their LDAP display names, select the appropriate name and open the property dialog to display the common name.

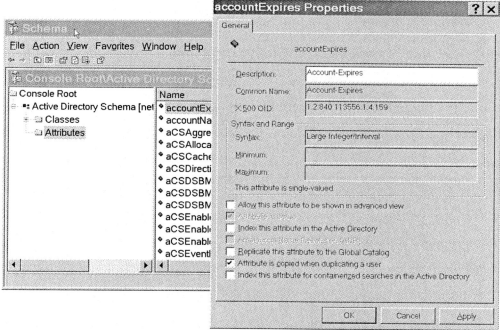

Figure D.1 – Attribute LDAP display name to common name mapping

You can map between the names using LDP, order the data using Sort Keys or Virtual List View.

To create this documentation we used csvde.exe to export the mappings between the attribute common names and the attribute LDAP display names. We created a script that returns the DN, the CN and the LDAP display name into a comma separated file. The file can be manipulated with a CSV editor such as Microsoft® Excel®.

The command string must be on a single line:

```
csvde -f details.csv -d
"cn=schema,cn=configuration,dc=example,dc=com"
-r "(objectClass=classSchema)"  -l "cn,lDAPDisplayName"
pause
```

Name Mapping

The mapping between LDAP display names and common names in most cases is fairly obvious (some are more obscure) and mainly involves the addition of a hyphen or two. The LDAP Display Name drops the initial capital letter and concatenates the words preserving the remaining capitalization. There are over 1000 attribute names returned when the script is run on Microsoft® Windows® Server 2003.

This is a small extract from the result set that the script produced:

LDAP Display Name	Common Name
userSharedFolder	User-Shared-Folder
userSharedFolderOther	User-Shared-Folder-Other
userSMIMECertificate	User-SMIME-Certificate
userWorkstations	User-Workstations

Some less obvious mappings that are listed below.

LDAP Display Name	Common Name
c	Country-Name
cn	Common-Name
co	Text-Country
dc	Domain-Component
directReports	Reports
homePhone	Phone-Home-Primary
info	Comment
l	Locality-Name
mail	E-mail-Addresses
memberOf	Is-Member-Of-DL
mobile	Phone-Mobile-Primary
name	RDN

LDAP Display Name	Common Name
notes	Additional-Information
o	Organization-Name
otherFacsimileTelephoneNumber	Phone-Fax-Other
otherHomePhone	Phone-Home-Other
otherIpPhone	Phone-Ip-Other
otherTelephone	Phone-Office-Other
ou	Organizational-Unit-Name
ownerBL	ms-Exch-Owner-BL
pager	Phone-Pager-Primary
sn	Surname
st	State-Or-Province-Name
street	Street-Address
streetAddress	Address
url	WWW-Page-Other

Appendix E – *userAccountControl* Flags

Account Control Flags

The *userAccountControl* is an attribute on account objects that specifies flags which define the behaviour of the account. The flags are defined in the SDK header file lmaccess.h and are summarized below.

If you are setting a value for the *userAccountControl* attribute either programmatically using ADSI or LDP you must add up the numeric values of all the flags that you require. The flag values are shown in hex but you must specify the value in decimal. Use the Microsoft® Windows® calculator in scientific mode to convert between hex and decimal.

Here's an example of the use of the flags for a normal account.

Required flags	Hex	Decimal
Normal account	0x200	512
Normal account + disabled	0x200 + 0x0002	514
Normal account + smartcard required	0x200 + 0x40000	262656

User Account Control Flags	Hex Value
UF_SCRIPT	0x0001
UF_ACCOUNTDISABLE	0x0002
UF_HOMEDIR_REQUIRED	0x0008
UF_LOCKOUT	0x0010
UF_PASSWD_NOTREQD	0x0020
UF_PASSWD_CANT_CHANGE	0x0040
UF_ENCRYPTED_TEXT_PASSWORD_ALLOWED	0x0080
UF_TEMP_DUPLICATE_ACCOUNT	0x0100
UF_NORMAL_ACCOUNT	0x0200
UF_INTERDOMAIN_TRUST_ACCOUNT	0x0800
UF_WORKSTATION_TRUST_ACCOUNT	0x1000
UF_SERVER_TRUST_ACCOUNT	0x2000
UF_DONT_EXPIRE_PASSWD	0x10000
UF_MNS_LOGON_ACCOUNT	0x20000
UF_SMARTCARD_REQUIRED	0x40000
UF_TRUSTED_FOR_DELEGATION	0x80000
UF_NOT_DELEGATED	0x100000
UF_USE_DES_KEY_ONLY	0x200000
UF_DONT_REQUIRE_PREAUTH	0x400000
UF_PASSWORD_EXPIRED	0x800000
UF_TRUSTED_TO_AUTHENTICATE_FOR_DELEGATION	0x1000000

Appendix F – Locale Identifiers

Locale identifier (LCID)	Default code page	Language: sublanguage
0x0436	1252	Afrikaans: South Africa
0x041c	1250	Albanian: Albania
0x1401	1256	Arabic: Algeria
0x3c01	1256	Arabic: Bahrain
0x0c01	1256	Arabic: Egypt
0x0801	1256	Arabic: Iraq
0x2c01	1256	Arabic: Jordan
0x3401	1256	Arabic: Kuwait
0x3001	1256	Arabic: Lebanon
0x1001	1256	Arabic: Libya
0x1801	1256	Arabic: Morocco
0x2001	1256	Arabic: Oman
0x4001	1256	Arabic: Qatar
0x0401	1256	Arabic: Saudi Arabia
0x2801	1256	Arabic: Syria
0x1c01	1256	Arabic: Tunisia
0x3801	1256	Arabic: U.A.E.
0x2401	1256	Arabic: Yemen
0x042b	Unicode only	Armenian: Armenia
0x082c	1251	Azeri: Azerbaijan (Cyrillic)
0x042c	1250	Azeri: Azerbaijan (Latin)
0x042d	1252	Basque: Spain
0x0423	1251	Belarusian: Belarus
0x0402	1251	Bulgarian: Bulgaria
0x0403	1252	Catalan: Spain
0x0c04	950	Chinese: Hong Kong SAR, PRC (Traditional)
0x1404	950	Chinese: Macau SAR (Traditional)
0x0804	936	Chinese: PRC (Simplified)
0x1004	936	Chinese: Singapore (Simplified)
0x0404	950	Chinese: Taiwan (Traditional)
0x0827	1257	Classic Lithuanian: Lithuania
0x041a	1250	Croatian: Croatia
0x0405	1250	Czech: Czech Republic
0x0406	1252	Danish: Denmark
0x0813	1252	Dutch: Belgium

Locale identifier (LCID)	Default code page	Language: sublanguage
0x0413	1252	Dutch: Netherlands
0x0c09	1252	English: Australia
0x2809	1252	English: Belize
0x1009	1252	English: Canada
0x2409	1252	English: Caribbean
0x1809	1252	English: Ireland
0x2009	1252	English: Jamaica
0x1409	1252	English: New Zealand
0x3409	1252	English: Philippines
0x1c09	1252	English: South Africa
0x2c09	1252	English: Trinidad
0x0809	1252	English: United Kingdom
0x0409	1252	English: United States
0x3009	1252	English: Zimbabwe
0x0425	1257	Estonian: Estonia
0x0438	1252	Faeroese: Faeroe Islands
0x0429	1256	Farsi: Iran
0x040b	1252	Finnish: Finland
0x080c	1252	French: Belgium
0x0c0c	1252	French: Canada
0x040c	1252	French: France (Standard)
0x140c	1252	French: Luxembourg
0x180c	1252	French: Monaco
0x100c	1252	French: Switzerland
0x042f	1251	FYRO Macedonian
0x0437	Unicode only	Georgian: Georgia
0x0c07	1252	German: Austria
0x0407	1252	German: Germany (Standard)
0x1407	1252	German: Liechtenstein
0x1007	1252	German: Luxembourg
0x0807	1252	German: Switzerland
0x0408	1253	Greek: Greece
0x0447	Unicode only	Gujarati: India
0x040d	1255	Hebrew: Israel
0x0439	Unicode only	Hindi: India
0x040e	1250	Hungarian: Hungary
0x040f	1252	Icelandic: Iceland
0x0421	1252	Indonesian: Indonesia

Locale identifier (LCID)	Default code page	Language: sublanguage
0x0410	1252	Italian: Italy (Standard)
0x0810	1252	Italian: Switzerland
0x0411	932	Japanese: Japan
0x044b	Unicode only	Kannada: India
0x0457	Unicode only	Konkani: India
0x0412	949	Korean (Extended Wansung): Korea
0x0440	1251	Kyrgyz: Kyrgyzstan
0x0426	1257	Latvian: Latvia
0x0427	1257	Lithuanian: Lithuania
0x083e	1252	Malay: Brunei Darussalam
0x043e	1252	Malay: Malaysia
0x044e	Unicode only	Marathi: India
0x0450	1251	Mongolian: Mongolia
0x0414	1252	Norwegian: Norway (Bokmål)
0x0814	1252	Norwegian: Norway (Nynorsk)
0x0415	1250	Polish: Poland
0x0416	1252	Portuguese: Brazil
0x0816	1252	Portuguese: Portugal
0x0446	Unicode only	Punjabi: India
0x0418	1250	Romanian: Romania
0x0419	1251	Russian: Russia
0x044f	Unicode only	Sanskrit: India
0x0c1a	1251	Serbian: Serbia (Cyrillic)
0x081a	1250	Serbian: Serbia (Latin)
0x041b	1250	Slovak: Slovakia
0x0424	1250	Slovenian: Slovenia
0x2c0a	1252	Spanish: Argentina
0x400a	1252	Spanish: Bolivia
0x340a	1252	Spanish: Chile
0x240a	1252	Spanish: Colombia
0x140a	1252	Spanish: Costa Rica
0x1c0a	1252	Spanish: Dominican Republic
0x300a	1252	Spanish: Ecuador
0x440a	1252	Spanish: El Salvador
0x100a	1252	Spanish: Guatemala
0x480a	1252	Spanish: Honduras
0x080a	1252	Spanish: Mexico
0x4c0a	1252	Spanish: Nicaragua

Locale identifier (LCID)	Default code page	Language: sublanguage
0x180a	1252	Spanish: Panama
0x3c0a	1252	Spanish: Paraguay
0x280a	1252	Spanish: Peru
0x500a	1252	Spanish: Puerto Rico
0x0c0a	1252	Spanish: Spain (Modern Sort)
0x040a	1252	Spanish: Spain (Traditional Sort)
0x380a	1252	Spanish: Uruguay
0x200a	1252	Spanish: Venezuela
0x0441	1252	Swahili: Kenya
0x081d	1252	Swedish: Finland
0x041d	1252	Swedish: Sweden
0x0444	1251	Tatar: Tatarstan
0x044a	Unicode only	Telgu: India
0x041e	874	Thai: Thailand
0x041f	1254	Turkish: Turkey
0x0422	1251	Ukrainian: Ukraine
0x0820	1256	Urdu: India
0x0420	1256	Urdu: Pakistan
0x0843	1251	Uzbek: Uzbekistan (Cyrillic)
0x0443	1250	Uzbek: Uzbekistan (Latin)
0x042a	1258	Vietnamese: Vietnam

Practical Techniques and Examples Index

Index

numerics

A

B

C

Figures